Volume 35

ADVANCES IN LIBRARIANSHIP: CONTEXTS FOR ASSESSMENT AND OUTCOME EVALUATION IN LIBRARIANSHIP

Advances in
Librarianship

Volume 35

ADVANCES IN LIBRARIANSHIP: CONTEXTS FOR ASSESSMENT AND OUTCOME EVALUATION IN LIBRARIANSHIP

Advances in
Librarianship

Edited by

Anne Woodsworth

Glen Cove, New York, USA

W. David Penniman

Columbus, Ohio, USA

United Kingdom • North America • Japan
India • Malaysia • China

Emerald Group Publishing Limited
Howard House, Wagon Lane, Bingley BD16 1WA, UK

First edition 2012

Reprints and permission service
Contact: permissions@emeraldinsight.com

British Library Cataloguing in Publication Data
A catalogue record for this book is available from the British Library

ISBN: 978-1-78190-060-4
ISSN: 0065-2830 (Series)

ISOQAR certified
Management Systems,
awarded to Emerald for
adherence to Quality
and Environmental
standards ISO 9001:2008
and 14001:2004,
respectively

Certificate Number 1985
ISO 9001
ISO 14001

INVESTOR IN PEOPLE

Contents

Documenting the Results of Good Intentions: Applying Outcomes Evaluation to Library Services for Children   47
Virginia A. Walter

Needs Analyses and Results

Assessment in a Medium-Sized Academic Library: A Success Story   65
Carolyn Gutierrez and Jianrong Wang

Using Needs Assessment to Develop Research and Grant Support Services   83
Ricardo R. Andrade and Christine E. Kollen

The Relationship between Collection Strength and Student Achievement   113

Rachel Wexelbaum and Mark A. Kille

Online Educational Case Studies

Learning Outcomes Assessment via Electronic Portfolios   135

Rachel Applegate and Marilyn M. Irwin

Evaluating Teaching in Online Programs: Comparing Faculty Self-Assessment and Student Opinion   151

Gail M. Munde

Contributors

Numbers in parentheses indicate the pages on which the author's contributions begin.

Ricardo R. Andrade (83), Libraries, The University of Arizona, Tucson, AZ, USA

Rachel Applegate (135), School of Library and Information Science, Indiana University, Indianapolis, IN, USA

Matthew Birnbaum (3), Office of Policy, Research and Evaluation, Institute of Museum and Library Services, Washington, DC, USA

Carolyn Gutierrez (65), Library, The Richard Stockton College of New Jersey, Galloway, NJ, USA

Marilyn M. Irwin (135), School of Library and Information Science, Indiana University, Indianapolis, IN, USA

Mark A. Kille (113), Free Geek, Portland, OR, USA

Christine E. Kollen (83), Libraries, The University of Arizona, Tucson, AZ, USA

Amanda R. Latreille (29), AmaLat Consulting, Elbridge, NY, USA

Gail M. Munde (151), Department of Library Science, College of Education, East Carolina University, Greenville, NC, USA

Kim Okahara (3), Office of Policy, Research and Evaluation, Institute of Museum and Library Services, Washington, DC, USA

Mary Ann Stiefvater (29), New York State Education Department/ New York State Library, Albany, NY, USA

Mary Linda Todd (29), New York State Education Department/New York State Library, Albany, NY, USA

Virginia A. Walter (47), Graduate School of Information and Library Science, University of California, Los Angeles, CA, USA

Jianrong Wang (65), Library, The Richard Stockton College of New Jersey, Galloway, NJ, USA

Mallory Warner (3), Office of Policy, Research and Evaluation, Institute of Museum and Library Services, Washington, DC, USA

Rachel Wexelbaum (113), Department of Information Media, School of Education, St. Cloud University, St. Cloud, MN, USA

Preface

Assessment and evaluation have become increasingly important in the nonprofit sector. Although initially used mostly in educational contexts to measure student learning, the strategy has migrated to other contexts such as measuring overall organizational and institutional successes, and the impact of projects, programs, and operational changes. This growing emphasis is in part due to increasingly stringent requirements imposed by government agencies, foundations, and other funding sources seeking to ensure that their investments result in significant impacts. In addition, the current economic climate and retrenchments in nonprofit agencies including colleges, universities, and public libraries have raised the need for assessment and outcomes evaluation to a critical level.

Assessment and evaluation are part of most individuals' daily lives. Sometimes these processes are simple and easy, like determining the edibility of a piece of fruit and the benefits derived from eating it. Sometimes they are complex, affected by social norms, laws, political influences, financial gain and loss, or environmental awareness. For example, if a city's government had to decide whether or not to approve establishment of a waste disposal processing plant within its boundaries, the impact on individual health as well as economic benefits from getting more taxes in its coffers, and the prospects of increased employment opportunities would be some of the important factors to consider. As assessment and evaluation began to be applied to the nonprofit and public sectors, the processes became more difficult and complex.

In the early stages of its development in education, assessment began with attempts to understand what students "knew" and could "do" as a result of their learning. To some extent, libraries have focused most evaluation efforts on development of tools with which to measure the impact of their information literacy and other instructional programs on their users—which for academic and public libraries, included students as well. The wealth of assessment tools now available is well document by Blevens (2012) who describes commercially administered ones as well as those developed by various other types of institutions. Blevens also points out additional resources such as the large collections of web resources hosted by the

University of North Carolina State University and at the National Institute for Learning Outcomes Assessment Organization's site housed at the University of Illinois in Urbana-Champaign, IL.

Prior to the mid-1990s, when the United Way of America led the way in nonprofit program evaluation, the norm was for librarian-generated standards to be the backbone for measuring the quality of library services and programs. To a great degree such guidelines or standards continue to be promulgated around the world. However, there has been a shift, somewhat to accommodate the emergence of electronic and web-based resources and environments as well as the need to demonstrate effective results from library activities and efforts. Large organizations such as the Chartered Institute of Library and Information Professionals (cilip) in the United Kingdom and the American Library Association (ALA) and its component divisions continue to produce guidelines and standards for service to all types of client groups but are moving focus to evaluate outcomes and document impact. EDUCAUSE, for example, developed a standard web-based survey to assist with collection of highly comparable performance measures for IT and libraries called Measuring Information Service Outcomes (MISO) (Consiglio, Allen, Baker, Creamer, & Wilson, 2011). EDUCAUSE (n.d.) also maintains an online collection of assessment and evaluation resources.

Determining needs and living with methodological constraints and challenges such as budget and time are critical to any evaluation efforts. Obviously, the *use* of the results from needs assessments and evaluations are key. In December 2011, *Library Journal* (LJ) hosted a Directors' Summit (Miller, Fialkoff, & Kelley, 2012) at which it was admitted by participants that while outputs provide "hard" data about library growth and use, there is need to demonstrate to funders and other stakeholders the underlying value and impact of libraries in their communities. Hence the arduous search for "squishy" outcomes, the term used by LJ's participants.

This volume is devoted to those "squishy" outcomes.

The lead chapter by Matthew Birnbaum, Kim Okahara, and Mallory Warner from the Institute of Museum and Library Services (IMLS) points the way toward the future evolution of assessments by organizations and their constituent parts, taking us beyond the now seasoned model of outcomes based evaluation and exploring a new approach to assessment. The authors bring into account the summative impact of IMLS in the United States in terms of their grants to libraries and contributions to the public good. From there the paper explores the relative benefits of nonlinear logic maps and emphasizes the importance of scaling evaluation from individual projects towards clusters of similar library services and activities across geographic areas. As they point out in their abstract, the authors provide a new perspective for library evaluation that moves from narrow methodological measures to broader administrative issues including diffusion of library use, effective integration of systematic data into program planning and administration, and strengthening multi-stakeholder communication.

Taking the topic to the state level, Amanda R. Latreille, consultant, with Mary Ann Stiefvater and Mary Linda Todd, staff members at the NY State Library's Development Office, describe how a majority of librarians in the state were trained in how to use evaluation methods at the working level in all types of libraries. In leading a top-down and statewide training program, they provide a model which can be utilized at many levels and throughout many disciplines and organizations. New York state, with a population of nearly 20 million, has over 750 public libraries with 1069 outlets, 270 academic libraries, 5400 school libraries as well as more than 1800 special libraries, making it an ideal test bed for library related studies and diffusion of knowledge (see http://www.nysl.nysed.gov/libdev/libs/stats.htm for 2010 statistics). Following these two chapters is an overview by Virginia A. Walter, Professor Emerita at the University of California, Los Angeles, and its Department of Information Studies. She recounts how outcome evaluation came into being across the United States for library services specifically geared to children and young adults—a movement for which she was instrumental and a leading light. Her historical review is brought to life with an "on the ground" example through a case study about its growth and acceptance in California state as a whole.

The next section of the volume, entitled "Needs Analyses and Results," begins with a chapter by Carolyn Gutierrez and Jianrong Wang from the Library at The Richard Stockton College of New Jersey, NJ. They provide a clear view into real situations by giving readers much to replicate and to think about. They further demonstrate how assessments impact library operations and effectiveness. Two LibQUAL+$^{®}$ surveys results were used to track trends and highlight the strengths and weaknesses of the library through the eyes of end users. Follow up user surveys indicated that, while library service improvements were made, user expectations rose even faster. From initial needs assessments through communication of results to all stakeholders the chapter proves that even small- to medium-sized libraries can implement assessment and evaluate outcomes in order to improve services. As Gutierrez and Wang point out, there is little need for statistical in-house expertise but a lot of need for campus-wide communication.

Ricardo R. Andrade and Christine E. Kollen from The University of Arizona, Tucson, AZ not only provide an informative case study of how to research and plan new services in general, but also serve up a model for how all types of libraries should plan for change, particularly in how best to involve stakeholders. They report on extensive assessments done to develop and improve library services in support of campus-wide research and grant activities and thus address institutional goals. They describe a process for change implementation which is much more important than evaluation for its own sake. The importance of their change model lies in its ability to be replicated in any size and type of library.

The third chapter in this section, by Rachel Wexelbaum (Collection Management Librarian at St. Cloud University, St.Cloud, MN) and Mark A. Kille (Human Resources Administrator, at Free Geek, Portland, OR), brings an important lesson to bear on the impact of collections on end users— despite the negative findings of their research. They found that prior research on the topic was sparse, to put it mildly. To wit, there is a desperate need for research and literature on two topics: (a) what students take away and use or internalize after they graduate and (b) what roles library collections and services play in development of long-term effects on students as a result of their learning. Both topics singly and in combination are ripe for dissertations and longitudinal studies by librarians, educators, sociologists, and other scholars. This chapter also emphasizes the importance of collaboration between library leadership and their clients.

The last section of the volume presents two case studies from the educational side of librarianship. These studies cover the use of online portfolios and how faculty and student evaluations compare with one another. Rachel Applegate and Marilyn M. Irwin from Indiana University's School of Library and Information Science, Indianapolis, IN provide real-world assessment tools with emphasis on electronic portfolio development as a means to program level assessment and improvements. Since most accreditation agencies require that student learning outcomes are assessed for every academic program and that the data gathered is used for continuous improvement of programs, this chapter provides a detailed model for doing so in online teaching environments.

Gail M. Munde, from the Department of Library Science at East Carolina University in Greenville, NC, presents a replicable and scalable method for assessment in an online teaching environment and supplies an excellent approach to assessment for online teaching and learning. Her analysis determined the level of agreement between faculty self-assessment and student assessment, in areas of overall program strength and directions for individual and whole-group professional development. The chapter contributes a method that (a) is replicable, scalable, (b) demonstrates that data are relatively easy to acquire, and (c) needs only basic statistical tests and measures for analysis. Since there are few studies that compare students' teaching evaluations with faculty self-evaluations, and none that specifically address these factors for library and information science education programs, this chapter provides an important analysis to the literature.

As editors, our heartfelt thanks go to the authors for enabling our work through being prompt with their submissions and highly responsive to our questions and suggestions. Members of the editorial advisory board deserve special thanks for giving us advice about the theme of the volume, for suggesting potential authors to us, and for reviewing submissions. The members are: Barbara Genco, editor of Collection Management at *Library Journal*, New York, NY; Tula Giannini, dean of the School of Information and Library Science at Pratt Institute, Brooklyn and New York, NY; Kenneth Haycock, Professor Emeritus and coordinator of the Center for Research and Innovations at San Jose's School of Library and Information Science, San Jose, CA; Maureen Mackenzie, associate professor of Management and Leadership at Dowling College, Oakdale, NY; Pat Molholt, Columbia University, New York, NY (retired); Marie Radford, associate professor at Rutgers University's School of Communication and Information in Newark, NJ; Robert A. Seal, dean of libraries at Loyola University, Chicago, IL; and last but not least, Barbara A. Stripling, who joined the board while in transition from the New York City School system as director of school library programs to becoming an assistant professor of practice at Syracuse University's School of Information Studies in Syracuse, NY.

Once again, our gratitude extends to the staff at Emerald, initially Diane Heath who moved on to lead another part of the company, and latterly Virginia Chapman our commissioning editor and her capable coworker, Catriona Gelder. It is a delight to have such capable and responsive support from them throughout the lengthy process of receiving and editing submissions.

References

Blevens, C. L. (2012). Catching up with information literacy assessment: Resources for program evaluation. *College & Research Libraries News* 73(4), 202–206.

cilip (n.d.). Retrieved from http://www.cilip.org.uk/get-involved/special-interest-groups/youth/publications/children/Pages/primaryguidelines.aspx

Consiglio, D., Allen, L., Baker, N., Creamer, K. J. T., & Wilson, J. (2011). Evaluating IT and library services with the MISO survey. *ECAR Research Bulletin 10*. Retrieved from http://www.educause.edu/Resources/EvaluatingITandLibrary Services/232855

EDUCAUSE. (n.d.). Boulder, CO: EDUCAUSE. Retrieved from http://www.educause.edu/resources

Miller, R., Fialkoff, F., & Kelley, M. (2012). *Data-driven libraries: Moving from outputs to outcomes*. Retrieved from http://lj.libraryjournal.com/2012/01/managing-libraries/data-driven-libraries-moving-from-outputs-to-outcomes/

Anne Woodsworth

W. David Penniman

Editors

The Broad View

Changes in Library Evaluation: Responding to External Pressures in the Institution of Museum and Library Services' *Measuring Success Initiative* for the Grants to States Program

Matthew Birnbaum, Kim Okahara and Mallory Warner
Office of Policy, Research and Evaluation, Institute for
Museum and Library Services, Washington, DC, USA

Abstract

This chapter examines the challenges of developing and implementing a new national evaluation approach in a complex library funding program. The approach shifts a prior outcome-based evaluation legacy using logic models to one relying on nonlinear logic mapping. The new approach is explored by studying the *Measuring Success* initiative, launched in March 2011 for the largest funded library services program in the United States, the Institute for Museum and Library Services formula-based Grants to States program. The chapter explores the relative benefits of nonlinear logic maps and emphasizes the importance of scaling evaluation from individual projects toward clusters of similar library services and activities. The introduction of this new evaluation approach required a new conceptual frame, drawing on diffusion, strategic planning, and other current evaluation theories. The new approach can be widely generalized to many library services, although its focus is on a uniform interorganizational social network embedded in service delivery. The chapter offers a new evaluation perspective for library service professionals by moving from narrow methodological concerns involving measurement to broader administrative issues including diffusion of library use, effective integration of systematic data into program planning and management, and strengthening multi-stakeholder communication.

Keywords: Results-based management; logic models; logic mapping; systems theory; diffusion; social networks

CONTEXTS FOR ASSESSMENT AND OUTCOME EVALUATION IN LIBRARIANSHIP
ADVANCES IN LIBRARIANSHIP, VOL. 35
© 2012 by Emerald Group Publishing Limited
ISSN: 0065-2830
DOI: 10.1108/S0065-2830(2012)0000035004

I. Introduction

The US political environment creates intense competition for social services and informal learning at all levels of government. This is not expected to change in the foreseeable future given economic circumstances. Evaluation research may be the most effective tool to help libraries respond to ever-changing technology demands, expanding diversity, and rapidly changing social needs in this political–economic environment.

The Institute for Museum and Library Services (IMLS) grant programs have incorporated program evaluation for about 15 years, but the practice remains nascent when compared to that of related sectors such as education, social services, and public health. Improving the quality and usefulness of library program evaluation requires a cultural shift in how the field approaches planning for the programs it plans and administers, and the role of assessment in both.

Library educators, executives, and professionals must alter the customs embedded by a prior generation of evaluation models. Lacking any straight-forward blueprint for change, this shift requires continuous adaptation to enable and sustain clearer articulation and understanding of what library programs intend and what actually happens. Constrained library budgets, increased demand for library services, and heightened requirements for persuasive evidence of tangible results exacerbate the need.

This chapter describes an initiative by IMLS and its state grant partners to revise program evaluation protocols for the largest US-funded library services program, formula grants to State Library Administrative Agencies (SLAAs), the Grants to States program under the Library and Services Technology Act (LSTA). The authors and collaborators have led this initiative, *Measuring Success*, since its inception in March 2011.

The next section summarizes the theory shaping the initiative. The subsequent section describes progress of *Measuring Success* to date. The final section offers lessons learned to guide future evaluation research and practice in library services.

A. Theoretical Background

Program evaluation includes more than monitoring and measurement. It involves systematic thinking about a program, raising meaningful questions, gathering and assessing evidence to provide answers, and applying all to strengthen a program (Russ-Eft & Preskill, 2009). There are as many approaches to program evaluation as to library program administration. Library programs are dynamic and continuously shaped by external influences; useful evaluation also relies on the capacity of library program administrators to effectively adapt. When external influences shift substantially enough, the evaluation approach also must change to retain value. Two primary reasons may make an evaluation approach stagnant and ineffective, consequently requiring adaptation. First, people act surrounded by uncertainties, and as in other areas of society, the knowledge base changes continuously. A 10-year-old "best practice" may no longer reflect the strongest current possibilities. Second, people resist change. Innovation takes effort. Repeated and significant change can cause burn out, compromising the effectiveness of an evaluation approach selected in the past.

Federal emphasis on evaluation started in the late 1960s with the growth of Great Society Programs (see, e.g., Weiss, 1972). Evaluation practice matured as part of a larger public administrative shift toward "results-based management," known more commonly in library services as "outcome-based evaluation" (OBE) (see, e.g., Rossi, Lipsey, & Freeman, 2004). OBE followed a similar trajectory in other public and nonprofit settings around the world, introducing new public management approaches that sought to better integrate business practice to governmental settings (see, e.g., Boston, Martin, Pallot, & Walsh, 1996).

1. Outcome-Based Evaluation

A major emphasis of OBE was to turn attention away from strict monitoring of whether funds were spent appropriately and protocols followed properly. This "input" approach to management was replaced by a private sector concern with bottom line results. The private sector challenge in prioritizing results ultimately boils down to maximizing profits, but the core philosophy driving the public and nonprofit sectors' bottom line focuses on beneficial changes to the public, and particularly to segments of the public that are targeted because they share a specific need.

As the new approach to public administration matured, OBE, tightly interwoven with logic models, became a dominant feature of the evaluation landscape in the US government and elsewhere. Multiple federal agencies, and philanthropic organizations such as the Centers for Disease Control and the United Way, have been in the forefront of this approach for several decades. It has remained the dominant federal approach since the 1990s in response to directives by the federal Office of Management and Budget (OMB) and the White House, associated with the Government Performance and Results Act of 1993 (GPRA). Consequently IMLS began to introduce OBE and logic models to their grantee communities as key tools for planning and evaluation by the latter part of that decade.

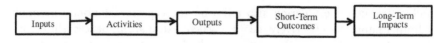

Fig. 1   Basic logic model structure.

The features of the basic logic model are easy to understand. A set of program "inputs" like labor, funding, and capital are allocated. Inputs shape program "activities" (or services). The activities lead to products or "outputs," which in turn lead to "outcomes" (see Fig. 1).

Generally, outcomes constitute immediate changes in program participants. Over time, longer-term outcomes, if they are sustained and shared with larger populations, are expected to create more sweeping changes in participants, communities, and/or other segments of society—these are often called impacts. Once a program logic model is complete, metrics are developed to assess whether projected changes in outputs, outcomes, and, ideally, impacts, happen and to what extent.

Consider an early child literacy program. A logic model articulates program intentions. Funds and staff are allotted as inputs. Staff designs and administers activities like curriculum design, instructor training, and outreach. These activities lead to an output of direct participation for pre-school or very early readers (and usually caregivers). As a result of participation, the children are expected, for instance, to increase their cognitive capacities and/or to become better prepared to participate in schooling. It is anticipated that the participating children will experience longer-term improvements in learning and higher academic success (impacts). Once a logic model and its embedded theory are complete, metrics can assess the validity for any included propositions. For instance, output metrics might count the number of participating children. Outcome metrics might estimate changes in participating children's cognitive abilities during the program's life.

The logic model approach is useful for program planning and assessment. It helps practitioners clarify program intentions by articulating an underlying logic. It helps frame data for collection and analysis. It moves administrator and policy maker focus to program performance by shifting attention from inputs and toward outputs, outcomes, and impacts.

2. OBE Weaknesses

Unfortunately, the model has four major weaknesses. First, the linear design can oversimplify the projected sequence of change in a frequently nonlinear world. Second, the model does not test alternative explanations or contradictions. At best, it recognizes external influences. Third, in practice the model generally lists *arrays* of potentially causal items under the various headings (inputs, activities, outputs, outcomes, and impacts), complicating both theoretical program logic and its subsequent assessment. Fourth, the model presumes objectivity, but programs are often created and implemented through processes requiring political compromise among individuals with different ideological perspectives, interests, and influence, situated across different institutional settings (Weiss, 1995).

Despite its weaknesses, the logic model remains highly recommended and applied in the US government and elsewhere. Its terms have become part of the vernacular of global public administration. While many evaluators grumble openly about the model's limits, no cohesive alternative replaced it. A group of evaluation theorists and practitioners, many affiliated with the Systems Thinking Topical Interest Group in the American Evaluation Association, has begun to seed an alternative (see, e.g., Rogers, 2008, 2010). Current social science discussions surrounding complexity theory are moving away from the mechanistic features of the logic model and toward more subtle interweaving of program dynamics within a larger environment and embracing complexity theories. For instance Patton (2011) has introduced a framework for logic mapping using nonlinear interactions at individual, organizational, and societal levels.

Two limits of the logic model are significant for this chapter. First, the societal impact of most public programs is due to nonlinear "tipping points" (Gladwell, 2000; Schelling, 1971). These arise when individuals act based on their perceptions of others' experiences. As ideas gain traction among a segment, they reach a tipping point where others become increasingly willing to adopt the notion. Then the notion "sticks" and becomes part of common lore (Heath & Heath, 2007); diffusion happens quickly and at a large scale. Second, external factors frequently influence both a program and the responses of participating individuals. Programs do not operate in a vacuum; they must be considered within their larger environment.

3. Theories of Change

Both limits affect an important theoretical issue underlying IMLS's *Measuring Success* initiative. Library services and programs operate on an implicit "theory of change"[1] associated with informal learning. A prevailing

---

[1] A theory of change is a way to make assumptions about how some factors lead to some type of social (or other) change which is subject to assessment for evaluating its relative effectiveness. See, for instance, Schmitt (2007) and Harris (2005).

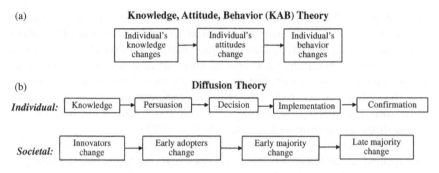

Fig. 2 Two informal learning theories of change.

interpretation of informal learning is based on variations of this theory of change: acquisition of some *knowledge* leads to *attitude* change that in turn leads to a change in *behavior*. The "KAB" theory of change (Fig. 2a) remains dominant in the social sciences and associated professional fields, including library services.

While elegant, KAB theory is overly simplistic. Social scientists and other learning theorists have invested substantial energies over decades to devise and test substantial refinements of KAB theory and others to understand how learning can lead to desired behavioral (or other types of) change. While nothing has yet removed the basic KAB theory from its pedestal, this is a central part of the arena.[2]

One leading alternative with supporting empirical evidence involves diffusion theory (see groundbreaking work of Rogers, 1962). This theory is illustrated in Fig. 2b. Diffusion theory works at both individual and societal levels. The top row of Fig. 2b focuses on individuals. Diffusion theorists divide individual learning change into five steps. First, an individual becomes aware of desirable *knowledge*. Then this person must be *persuaded* of its value. Once persuaded, the person must *decide* to access it (e.g., through program participation). Afterwards, the person must *implement* the knowledge (i.e., apply it) to validate usefulness to his/her circumstance. If the net benefit is positive, the individual ultimately *confirms* its personal value and

---

[2]Despite a wealth of literature in the public health and social psychology fields in the 1980s, not much empirical testing of the model has occurred. Many scholars have either qualified the model to better specify types of knowledge, attitudes, and behaviors involved or modified links. For a nice synopsis of the model and its shortfalls, see Farrior (2005).

adopts the desired behavioral change. In short, this model suggests that any program seeking to benefit individuals through *knowledge* must first persuade them that acquiring the knowledge is worthwhile, and then hope the individual decides it is valuable enough to sustain it through a behavioral change.

There are other applicable theories beyond KAB and diffusion. Using insights from strategic planning theory (Bryson, 2004), program staff contend with influences outside direct organizational control (external influences) in seeking to affect target populations. These involve "opportunities" and "threats" (or "barriers"). Consider again a library early childhood literacy program. Even if program staff appropriately target a group of families who could greatly benefit from such service, that group may not participate even if they agree gains will result. Their reasons may not be irrational but reflect perceived barriers like practical transportation access or childcare constraints. Conversely, innovations in information technology may offer new opportunities for participation in childhood literacy programs, even without changes in target group awareness of its benefits.

As Fig. 2b also shows, diffusion theory provides insight into how individual change can aggregate into societal change.[3] Using economic terminology, "spillovers" happen when something affects one individual and then spreads to another. Diffusion theorists articulate such spread by assuming that some individuals are more prone to lead and others to follow. While Rogers' (1962) diffusion theory described five types of individuals, people more realistically fall on a continuum. At one extreme, there are risk-takers willing to immediately adopt innovation, like participating in a new library program. Others, more cautious in varying degrees, will wait and assess others' experiences before opting to participate and adopt their learning to change their circumstances. At the far extreme are risk-adverse individuals who may never choose participation and potential change.[4] This aspect of diffusion theory is key in understanding how library programs can gradually increase popularity and impact; it is based on the continued intermingling of former, current, and potential participants and not just on the direct interactions between library staff and some clientele at one point in time.

---

[3]By societal change, we are simplifying multiple units of change that extend beyond individuals, such as distinct groups, communities, and so forth.

[4]Those with experience in organizational politics may have seen this referenced as the "80:20" rule. This means that change may never reach 20% of a target population.

II. IMLS Grants to States and the *Measuring Success* Initiative

We now turn our attention to the IMLS's *Measuring Success* initiative Grants to States.

A. The Political Context

There are three important policy features of IMLS Grants to States that have influenced choices for building a refined evaluation system. First, this has always been a formula-based federal program, resulting in complex intergovernmental relationships. The federal authorizing legislation places responsibility for the program's oversight in IMLS, but provides SLAAs with substantial discretion in the services and activities they carry out. Further, many SLAAs have redistributed a large share of funds to local public libraries through project grants to tailor services and programs to various communities. Consequently, three governmental actors interface—IMLS, the SLAAs, and local libraries. Much multilevel cooperation is needed. Perhaps reflecting the absence of regulatory laws, the level of intergovernmental cooperation between IMLS and the SLAAs always has been high.

Since the formal parameters of Grants to States have been shaped through the legislative process, like most such products, its intentions are purposely broad. The LSTA has always stated overarching purposes, such as rural library services, technology infrastructure, and more. Recently, library-to-library collaboration and library partnerships with nonlibrary organizations have been highlighted. The LSTA however has never articulated explicit outcomes through this program that are intended to benefit participant circumstances.

Third, LSTA legislation for Grants to States is tied to Congressional authorization for IMLS. Since the first Library Services bill was signed on June 19, 1956, each federal authorization has stipulated that each state receiving funding must provide a formal plan for its use. The federal government began to institute evaluation requirements in 1990. IMLS was created in 1996 with funding both the library and museum communities amalgamated in the Congressional legislation. That legislation required that each SLAA conduct an independent evaluation of the results of its five-year plan. Processes were left to each SLAA. The federal legislation however complicates fulfilling evaluation requirements due to a discontinuity in the timing of the required SLAA five-year plans and five-year evaluations. As a result, the five-year SLAA evaluations can only assess three to four years of their five-year plans. The evaluations and plans nonetheless are perceived as important contributors to transparency and to strengthening agency level performance at a federal level even if research strongly suggests that elected and appointed senior governmental policy makers rarely read the required evaluation reports (McDavid & Huse, 2012).

OBE based on logic models was first introduced to the Grants to States program in 1997 and applied through 2011. It is the focus of the next section.

III. Introduction of Logic Models to Grants to States: 1997—2011

Grants to States, like nearly every other public program, historically has focused its administrative oversight on monitoring inputs to ensure that funds have been spent properly. While the 1990 and 1996 federal legislation highlighted increased federal concern for monitoring outcomes, fiscal accountability has remained part of the dominant program culture.

As IMLS began to offer guidance and leadership in OBE to Grants to States in response to the federal evaluation directives, it had to balance several concerns. First, it had to balance the monitoring of inputs and their outcomes. Second, as a state formula grant program, it had to balance federal government interests versus those of state governments. Third, since many SLAA investments were made through project awards to local public libraries, any new type of evaluation approach introduced to Grants to States had to be integrated with project grant administration.

Against this backdrop, IMLS began to introduce OBE with logic models to the Grants to States program in 1997. It hired an evaluation officer and contracted with a third-party expert in program evaluation. Training workshops were introduced to participating SLAA partners in using logic models for planning and assessment of outcomes. Every state had to select at least one project for OBE assessment. IMLS staff, in turn, availed themselves to support SLAA capacity to undertake new and increased programmatic evaluative responsibilities.

While federal legislation required each SLAA to conduct a five-year evaluation, IMLS gave each the option to decide whether to include OBE and in what form. The SLAAs increasingly placed emphasis on their own project grants to public libraries. Some adopted a requirement for a simplified logic model and OBE in project grants to libraries, and some built tools and training for that purpose.

This move to OBE required changes in the IMLS Grants to States web-based annual reporting system. The focus remained at a project level, with much of the architecture continuing to monitor expended funds. This reporting system allowed OBE reporting for both the SLAA as a whole and for its project grants. Reporting progress made in building SLAA OBE capacity was optional, with more detailed information requested at the project level. Fields in the online reporting tool were created for projects to enter information on activities, outputs, and outcomes, paralleling logic model architecture.

Substantial effort was devoted to creating a taxonomy to classify projects related to legislated priorities, but no standardized measures at the project level were incorporated for outputs or outcomes. The reluctance to examine program participants' experiences in library programs reflected a hesitancy to cross a perceived user confidentiality barrier. It also reflected an inability to develop a logical structure to accommodate wide variation in service delivery.

As the effort to use this approach to OBE matured through a little over the first half of the decade, IMLS continued to invest substantial resources to this endeavor. This impacted relations with each SLAA partner, as a number of the states soon designated at least one staff person to manage the new OBE approach within their agency. Further, attempts were made to drill deeper into two specific areas involving substantive investment of Grants to States funds for project grants—early childhood reading and staff development. While analyses were done for guiding assessment and pilots launched in multiple sites around both subject areas, the endeavors were not brought to a level of refinement to support large-scale adoption.

Overall, the Grants to States reporting system evolved without a unified theory of change to cumulate results for the plethora of library programs supported with Grants to States funds across SLAAs and their local library partners. As a result, IMLS and its independent contractors for assessment of the SLAA five-year evaluations submitted in 2002 and 2007 found it extremely difficult to aggregate beyond individual projects to assess the performance of a state or a suite of libraries involved with the same program category (e.g., early childhood reading).

Evaluation became part of the vocabulary for IMLS and grantees, but the terms and evidence derived from its incorporation could not yet be used systematically to frame conceptual understandings or to guide high-level decisions. Instead, the SLAAs' autonomy, combined with disparate evaluation and program planning experience and knowledge across the Grants to States universe, created a system of complex and vaguely understood elements, fragmented across a multitude of projects. This made monitoring funding expenditures by project category complex and evaluation of results beyond individual projects nearly impossible.

By the latter part of the decade, a change in the appointed IMLS director corresponded with a de-emphasis in program evaluation in Grants to States (and elsewhere in the agency). The third-party evaluation training contract ended with no substitute. The one IMLS evaluation officer was reassigned and no replacement was hired. Remaining IMLS staff had never been never fully integrated for using OBE. Eventually IMLS stopped investing in improving its information reporting systems on the grounds of concerns for efficiency and the promise of government-wide solutions (which have not yet been implemented into this program's administration at the time of this writing).

Ultimately, as project-level OBE using logic models was integrated into Grants to States program administration, and pertinent new technical and administrative challenges emerged, funds and resources moved away. Little was learned about how Grants to States translated into impacts on the public.

Despite these shortcomings, this era is noteworthy for an unprecedented shift in the program culture with a deliberate linkage of planning with evaluation under the rubric of OBE with logic models. This linkage is important as it had influenced responsibilities within each SLAA as well as between IMLS and SLAAs. The adopted approach to OBE, despite its imperfections, gained a strong foothold in the Grants to States program.

This legacy would shape the parameters for the *Measuring Success* initiative, the focus of the next section.

IV. Impetus for the *Measuring Success* Initiative

By 2010, the political calculus across all levels of government had changed fundamentally. It became and remains politically risky to rely primarily on articulating the belief that fostering strong libraries nurtures a vibrant democracy as an argument for sustaining and expanding funding in this area. It has become imperative to move beyond this narrative by much better ability to demonstrate *how* public investments in library services result in concrete benefits to the public. In fact, while overall demand for library services has continued to increase, aggregate state funding for library services has shrunk (Institute for Museum and Library Services, 2011).

In alignment with the political realities that spur the new urgency to increase the evaluative capabilities in Grants to States, new IMLS leadership created an Office of Planning, Research, and Evaluation (OPRE). In addition to overseeing the agency's new statistical research program, this office is charged with oversight and reporting on IMLS programmatic performance.

To help meet these demands, new research and evaluation staff were hired, including a senior evaluation officer late in 2010 and a second evaluation officer in 2011. In early winter of 2011 IMLS's new appointed director signaled that evaluation was a chief priority of her administration. The LSTA Grants to States program, as the agency's largest single program, has been at the forefront of this new policy direction.

A new IMLS evaluation approach to Grants to States has required SLAA buy-in as partners to ground the content while preserving each state's flexibility to address the unique circumstances in their jurisdiction. It has required a more consistent framework to: (1) track performance of activities and services in the LSTA Grants to States over time and across different programmatic areas; (2) enable a much stronger performance synthesis that allows for purposeful clustering across individual projects; and (3) better identify and foster best practices and shared learning.

A. Designing the *Measuring Success* Initiative

Creating a new evaluation approach for this formula grant program has faced several key challenges. For better and worse, evaluation has been closely tied to logic models since the late 1990s, and severely decentralized at a project level. Key parties in IMLS and its SLAA grantees have had disparate understandings of evaluation and interpretations of definitions and application of project measures. Finally, any solution must be embedded in a new grant performance reporting system.

Following months of building internal consensus, a framework for restructuring the evaluation approach for Grants to States was shared with SLAA participants at their annual convening in March 2011. This new OBE approach moved away from logic models. Decisions were operationalized in two transparent principles. First, the development of the new evaluation approach would unfold iteratively and incrementally. Three overlapping phases to occupy an approximately 24-month period were delineated: design, pilot, and roll-out. Sequential steps within each phase would provide systematic points for reflection and adaptation as appropriate. Second, the process was designed to be participatory. States would drive the content while IMLS would take an active facilitating role. Additional external stakeholders, such as experts in methodology, would be brought in as circumstances warranted.

As the overriding vision for *Measuring Success* was communicated, attention turned toward the first phase in designing the new evaluation system. Four sequential steps were initially planned: (1) kick-off at the March 2011 meeting, (2) "backward logic mapping," (3) "forward logic mapping," and (4) creation of assessment frameworks. At this time, basic features of the new design are nearly complete and are the focus of the remainder of this section.

1. Kick-off

The March 2011 annual meeting of SLAA staff was comprised predominantly of SLAA directors (chiefs), state grant coordinators, and other senior SLAA professionals. The event was structured to engage the SLAAs as partners in a process with which participants had some familiarity. SLAA participants were broken into four groups/teams that reflected six of eight major priorities spelled out in the new federal legislation summarized in Table 1.[5]

Table 1
Federal Priorities of Grants to States Program

1. Expanding services for learning and access to information and educational resources in a variety of formats, in all types of libraries, for individuals of all ages in order to support such individuals' needs for education, lifelong learning, workforce development, and digital literacy skills.
2. Establishing or enhancing electronic and other linkages and improved coordination among and between libraries and entities ... for the purpose of improving the quality of and access to library and information services.
3. Providing training and professional development, including continuing education, to enhance the skills of the current library workforce and leadership, and advance the delivery of library and information services; and enhancing efforts to recruit future professionals to the field of library and information services.
4. Developing public and private partnerships with other agencies and community-based organizations.
5. Targeting library services to individuals of diverse geographic, cultural, and socioeconomic backgrounds, to individuals with disabilities, and to individuals with limited functional literacy or information skills.
6. Targeting library and information services to persons having difficulty using a library and to underserved urban and rural communities, including children ... from families with incomes below the poverty ... .
7. Developing library services that provide all users access to information through local, State, regional, national, and international collaborations and networks.
8. Carrying out other activities consistent with the purposes [of LSTA], as described in the State library administrative agency's plan.

[5]The IMLS team working on *Measuring Success* agreed that the fourth priority, partnerships, would be integrated in other priorities. It also was decided to omit the last

Each team contained about 25 SLAA participants and 2 IMLS facilitators. In beginning a new OBE approach that differed from logic models, the teams engaged in "backward logic mapping." Teams were assigned one or two of the federally authorized priorities for review and identification of key objectives. Participants next articulated and ranked the most important external opportunities outside of the program related to these objectives. The opportunities were vetted using a taxonomy that considered *political, economic, sociocultural,* and *technological* influences as distinct areas of external influence on the program (see Bryson, 2004, for details of the PEST taxonomy). In a subsequent activity, participants repeated the process for external programmatic barriers. Finally, participants began to list and prioritize strategies to address the opportunities and barriers they had now identified and ranked.

By day's end, the meeting rooms were filled with flip charts sprinkled with post-it notes and colored dots representing rankings of the opportunities, barriers, and strategies. The introduction of a single strategic planning tool, exercised in the same way across all of the SLAA/IMLS teams, moved participant preoccupation away from sensitive issues associated with state autonomy and changes in performance measurement and toward discussion of what the Grants to States program intended to achieve as a whole. It also helped build trust and common ground on the importance of moving forward to develop a new evaluation approach.

2. Continued Backward Logic Mapping

Communication between IMLS and SLAA partners continued following the conference. *Measuring Success* "branding" occurred with the creation of a Wiki. By late spring, SLAA participants had self-selected into six teams, each roughly corresponding to a priority in the new federal legislation.[6]

Webinars were held biweekly from late May through early July 2011. Teams completed backward logic maps correlated to the six federal priorities. They identified and recommended strategies to attain objectives associated with their priority, either directly or indirectly through "capturing" an opportunity or barrier. Fig. 3 illustrates a sample backward logic map produced during that time.

priority, since it allows the SLAAs to meet other nonspecified state library needs with Grants to States funds.

[6]Many team members participating in the webinar process had not participated in the March 2011 conference.

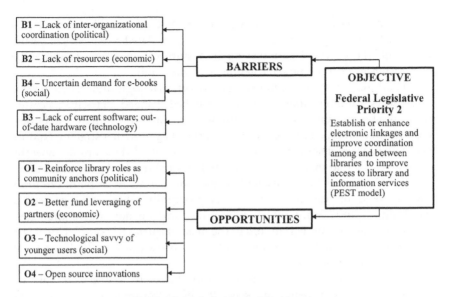

Fig. 3 Sample backward logic map.

The backward mapping efforts were most successful in identifying specific objectives and associated barriers and opportunities. They were less successful in articulating the logic by which a successful program could reach its objective. Sometimes the program and objective were considered identical. Other strategies focused on related efforts such as advocacy. While participants homed in on key opportunities and barriers that could affect achievement of a selected objective, it often remained unclear how a strategy or bundle of strategies could capture external opportunities or barriers to produce the desired result.

3. Forward Logic Mapping

By July, many SLAA participants were interacting frequently in various teams, virtually and by telephone. They included chiefs, senior librarians, and mid-level professionals.

In furthering momentum for emerging communities of practice (another underlying goal of the process), the teams began to use "forward logic mapping" to build out the new evaluation scheme. SLAA and IMLS participants referred to these logic maps as "results chains." Forward logic maps or results chains involved vetting a series of if/then statements.

Participants began with a strategy articulated toward the end of the backward logic map construction. They then postulated a sequence of events that could be expected culminating in a suite of outcomes changing the circumstances of some targeted segment of the public.

These results chains differed from traditional logic models in several major ways. Both terminology and concepts had changed. Participants ceased to think about change as a simple linear flow, connecting inputs, activities, outputs, outcomes, and impacts. Instead, they began with a strategy (and its associated subset of supporting activities), and proceeded to consider how the strategy could lead to a subsequent related, desired result. A result could lead to another result or to initiation of an additional strategy, or both. No limit was imposed on the number of strategies/results that could proceed a concluding result. Similarly, there was no limit on how many strategies/results might be needed to reach the next sequential point. This logic mapping accommodated many nonlinear interactions and allowed for recursive changes as well.

Social network theory also was introduced to frame and validate emerging theories of change in the results chains (for more on social network theory in evaluation, see, Penual, Sussex, & Korbak, 2006). Four sets of actors were identified: (1) SLAAs; (2) public libraries;[7] (3) *nonlibrary partners*; and finally, (4) users, comprising distinct segments from the broad public. Fig. 4 summarizes the underlying social network revealed across all of the results chains.

As seen in Fig. 4, the four sets of actors are closely interwoven. First, the SLAAs conduct needs assessments, develop long-term statewide plans, and extend available types of support to catalyze efforts among public libraries. Second, public libraries customize the planning to the circumstances of their communities, which subsequently leads to delivering pertinent services and activities to various segments of the local public. Third, outside partners bring expertise, capital, and connections to assist SLAA efforts at a state level as well as public libraries in their local communities. Fourth, users (i.e., segments of the public) access and participate in the library services and activities. As teams refined their chains, the social network was refined further to stratify users into two groups: target users who initially participate in the library services and activities, and potential users who might opt to participate in the same services and activities as target users diffuse information about value they found.

---

[7]Many states give project grants to different types of libraries. For the purposes of this chapter, however, the discussion is confined to public libraries, since it is this type of library that has been the predominant focus of discussion during the *Measuring Success* initiative.

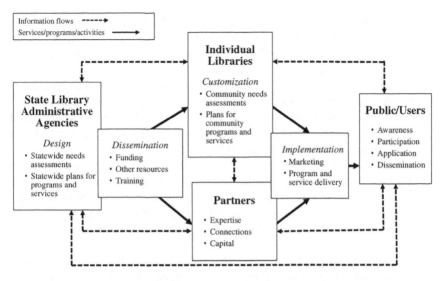

Fig. 4 Social network for grants to states.

By the end of this phase, each team had produced at least three results chains that corresponded with their perceptions of major objectives tied to their team's federal priority. The 6 teams completed about 25 results chains over a six-week period.

4. Refining Results Chains

As the initial iteration of the logic maps was finalized, this phase of SLAA teamwork ended. The initiative's original design had assumed that the logic mapping would be complete enough that SLAA planning participants could: (1) recommend points on the results chains for national assessment; and (2) agree on construction and methods of assessment at these points using descriptive statistics and/or other appropriate qualitative tools. The first goal was complete by mid-August, but the second never occurred. Instead, after reflection, it became clear that further refinement of the logic was needed.

Chain refinement reflected the political reality of federal legislation governing Grants to States. Its programmatic priorities did not articulate specific outcomes expected for various segments of the US public and communities. The initial round of results chains exposed a schism in mapping to federal priorities and to intended changes in participant circumstances. A decision consequently was made to continue IMLS facilitation of the new system design for another several months using a smaller group of SLAA participants who had emerged as leaders. Seventeen mid-level professionals from 16 SLAAs agreed to participate as technical advisors.

These technical advisors first convened in a webinar in late September 2011. A new configuration was presented for consideration. Table 2 shows how the 25 results chains created by the original SLA teams were organized into focal areas that reflected the types of library services that SLAAs typically support through Grants to States.

The technical advisors agreed on this classification scheme and moved to refine the original results chains better to delineate steps in the social network that lead to desired changes in different segments of the public (i.e., users). Ultimately, consensus emerged that staff and leadership development was best integrated into results chains for the other focal areas and best viewed as in interim outcome.

As the teams further refined the results chains by focal areas, they implicitly agreed to an emerging theory of change for informal learning as summarized in Fig. 5.

As seen in this figure, program staff make initial assessments of the potential target public in a community or catchment area. These assessments include not only the types of learning that can benefit specific segments of the public, but also external opportunities and barriers that are likely to influence public participation in the informal learning opportunity. Following assessment, efforts are made to directly enable informal learning for individuals and to address indirect opportunities and barriers that may influence the ability and/or desire to access an identified body of knowledge. In inducing individuals to participate in a library's learning program, attention is focused on capturing external opportunities and barriers through incentives. Finally, assuming satisfactory experience and effective incentives, the theory assumes initial target users will share their experience with others.

Table 2
Focal Areas for Programs and Services Typically Supported by IMLS Grants to States

1.	Lifelong learning
2.	Community services
3.	Employment and small business development
4.	Digitization
5.	Database delivery
6.	Civic engagement
7.	Staff and leadership development (distributed throughout other focal areas)

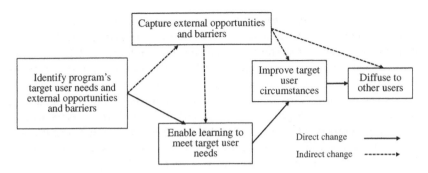

Fig. 5 Informal learning program theory of change.

These other users would adopt the same benefits acquired by the target users through diffusion. The one complexity not illustrated in Fig. 5 concerns that this programmatic action operates through a social network that interrelates an SLAA, public libraries, other potential partners, and a suite of distinct user groups.

The emerging theory of change moved participants away from both KAB and diffusion theory in making the causal link from acquiring knowledge to its subsequent application. As seen in Fig. 5, causality is embedded in capturing external opportunities or threats as the program interacts with the users. In practical terms, capturing these opportunities and threats involve applying appropriate incentives such as social media innovations or, say, addressing childcare constraints. This insight moved the program's theory of change further into social networking by building on insights of social marketing theorists such as Lefebvre (2010). Put simply, acquisition of knowledge may not suffice for someone to act or change behavior, be it in deciding to participate in some library service/activity or in subsequently applying the learning acquired from that participation to another aspect of the participant's life (e.g., applying and obtaining a job). Incentives matter. Further, diffusion is seen as an outgrowth of the process: as one individual experiences the benefits of participating in some library service or activity, spillovers are more likely to occur by either the target user opting to participate in another library program or another group of users opting to participate in the initial library program.

V. Creating an Assessment Framework

By early November 2011, the technical advisors had finished the bulk of their work. The teams had refined results chains for five focal areas (including online databases but excluding civic engagement). All incorporated the same set of interrelated actors in a social network and articulated a unified theory of change associated with informal learning. Unlike logic models, the results chains relied extensively on nonlinear relationships culminating in expected improvements for a plethora of groups in society.

As the new focal area results chains were finalized, the technical advisors moved to consider designing an assessment framework to measure whether the theories embedded in the results chain worked as intended, and if not, to be able to adapt and modify. Links on the results chains were reviewed to decide whether national assessment was merited. If the answer was yes, research questions were vetted around these links.

At this point, an unexpected challenge emerged. IMLS had always assumed that evaluation methods would not rely exclusively on statistical performance indicators. It expected that the nature of the question would drive the method, be it statistical metrics and/or other qualitative inquiry approaches. The senior author of this chapter led methods selection in close collaboration with the director of IMLS's Office for Planning, Research, and Evaluation. This task had been presumed to be relatively straightforward, given their education and experience, but it turned out otherwise.

If a new evaluation approach to collect data across disparate projects and connect to the interactive social network of the SLAA universe was to be created, an entirely new scheme that could scale across local, state, and national levels was needed. There was no precedent for such a system in library services in the United States. Besides introducing new political and social uncertainties into the newly emerging evaluation approach, this lack of precedent created a methodological complexity. It was one issue to ask SLAAs to report about matters to which they had direct control, such as funds allotted for a particular program category, say, through a project grant over a given time interval. It was something else to collect data for initiatives over which they have no direct control, and in which no dominant culture for using data in programmatic decision making exists (e.g., changes in employment status for participants in a library-based employment training program). A one-size-fits-all data assessment model was not possible.

As a result, the *Measuring Success* design phase stopped again for reflection in late fall 2011. By this time, the political urgency of the initiative had increased again, as the state library directors (chiefs) were scheduled to meet at one of their periodic meetings. Discussions between IMLS senior leadership and these state library officials at this meeting about progress already made led to renewed support to continue the *Measuring Success* endeavor.

The proposed solution for the assessment scheme was developed by IMLS internally in winter 2012. The schism in the earlier evaluation approach with logic models used in Grants to States between projects and some higher unit of analysis was resolved in the new evaluation approach by targeting the focal areas in the results chains as foundations. Using prior input from SLAA participants, projects were classified into discrete activities and services corresponding to each of the focal areas. This scheme would focus on performance across the entire social network, with discrete assessments of an SLAA, a participating library, and some targeted set of users. Another priority simplified the logic to enable easier aggregation of data across individual projects.

The process for building out the solution continued to rely on incremental change to strengthen capacity and buy-in of the SLAAs. Initially, reporting would not look much different from the present, but information would be simplified and streamlined. Annual reporting would retain the essential need to monitor expenditures, particularly at project levels, but it would improve the capacity to report outcomes, at least to the extent they could be attributed to IMLS funding to SLAAs and their local libraries. This reform also would begin to allow for better aggregation of information across individual projects.

A gradual build out of the whole assessment framework for user-specific impact would happen by piloting through volunteer SLAAs. Building this pilot capacity would foster participation in new communities of practice among participating states and their network. As their capacity increased, diffusion of new practices to other states would be more possible. In addition, data would be collected and analyzed across clusters of projects that corresponded with various activities under each of the focal areas.

The overall strategy introduced an additional new wrinkle. Instead of being confined to an annual SLAA web-based reporting system linked to mandates for five-year plans and evaluations for data collection and reporting, IMLS would exercise leadership and resources to frame multisite evaluations of selected activities and services within focal areas (e.g., evaluation of a suite of childhood reading projects across a suite of local libraries under the lifelong learning focal area).

A. Next Steps

At the time of writing, IMLS is vetting the design of the program's new evaluation system with its SLAA partners. Unlike in 2011, the 2012 conversations are more grounded, encompassing the discussions between IMLS and its SLAA partners over the past year around the completion of the design phase of the *Measuring Success* initiative. The planned design contains a more logical structure for detailing the plethora of initiatives for which SLAA partners use Grants to States funds. The system is built on the nonlinear unifying theories of change embedded in the results chains developed by IMLS and the SLAAs. It contains a more logical approach to measurement and assessment and enables individual projects to be systematically sorted into coherent clusters for higher-level assessments of particular library initiatives for each SLAA and the nation at large.

The plan also details next steps in the *Measuring Success* initiative, including a roll-out of a new performance reporting system and SLAA partners that have volunteered to pilot these innovations. The high level of collaboration using virtual and other technologies continues. Emphasis is placed on creating and nurturing new communities of practice, diffusion, reflection, and adaptation for continuous learning.

VI. Discussion

The authors expected that the flaws in logic models would manifest as a major lesson for participants in this initiative. This is believed to be true. Logic models have demonstrated limits. The approach adopted in *Measuring Success*, using backward and forward logic maps, has provided an effective alternative to IMLS's OBE architecture in allowing participants to better articulate the major types of library services and programs that libraries actually deliver using Grants to States funds. It allows for nonlinear relationships. Participants have embraced dynamic environmental interactions, leading to an emerging theory of change that embeds a social network of interdependent actors.

The approach using the backward and forward logic maps also had another intentional benefit. Logic models presented a simple and attractive way of integrating planning with assessment when OBE was initially introduced to Grants to States in 1997. The logic maps introduced in the *Measuring Success* initiative significantly increased the strength and quality of the integration. The logic maps focused explicitly on issues surrounding planning in better specifying precisely what the various activities captured in Grants to States' various focal areas intended to achieve in benefitting specific segments of the American public. Stakeholder acceptance of the new approach to outcome-based evaluation (or, more broadly, results-based management) resulted in large because of this greater capacity of logic mapping. Further, the increased quality of articulation of program intentions using the forward logic maps enabled the ability to develop a more sophisticated and clearer logic for assessment and measurement.

Nonetheless, logic models were only one challenge in changing an entire culture formed around prior program evaluation experiences. In particular, IMLS's evaluation approach in Grants to States decentralized data collection and analysis in individual project grants without systematic links to support broadly useful collection and analysis of data for state and federal decision making. Whether fortuitous or otherwise, the forward and backward logic maps in the *Measuring Success* initiative enabled development of solutions that allow scaling of individual projects into clusters of similar activities using the derived focal areas as a foundation. This foundation has led to construction of a logical reporting structure that should greatly increase the effectiveness of overall monitoring of expended funds and performance for individual projects when clustered into their hierarchical groupings. We anticipate it will be both more effective and more persuasive in showing the value of libraries to the public.

The capacity of the new evaluation approach to function more effectively across multiple levels was directly related to the introduction of systems theory thinking. A structured social network linking a suite of actors is critical for evaluating the effectiveness of a wide array of library services supported through Grants to States. The same is true for the introduction of environmental opportunities and threats as action points in program planning and monitoring. These precepts are essential for understanding the realities of any community-based program, with those of a local library a core example. They are expected to yield huge future dividends when stakeholders begin to consider applying evidence emerging from this new evaluation approach. There is huge potential for generalizing this insight to a slew of other library service endeavors grounded in rich community relationships.

A major factor that will determine the effectiveness of this new evaluation approach will be its usefulness to various stakeholders (Patton, 2008). The process used in launching *Measuring Success* has increased the likelihood of such success. SLAA participants can see their fingerprints on the entire scheme as they drove the content, with active IMLS leadership and fulfillment. With greater ownership of the product, the SLAA partners and IMLS program staff are more likely to value it, apply it, and find it more useful.

Technical, administrative, and political uncertainties remain. Prior habits that have shaped understanding about what evaluation entails, particularly the emphasis on tracking expended funds and assessing outcomes for individual and widely disparate projects remains a core mindset among many SLAA and IMLS staff despite the progress made over the past year with the launching of the *Measuring Success* initiative.

Change takes consistency, iteration, and time. The point of this case study is that change is historical. The changes made thus far in introducing a new OBE approach linking program planning with assessment would not have been possible if there had not been experience with a prior one using logic models. The prior approach reflected dominant professional thinking at the time of introduction 15 years ago. Correspondingly, even if progress continues in instituting a new evaluation approach to the Grants to States program, there undoubtedly will be unforeseen technical, administrative, and political uncertainties that will arise, requiring further reflection and adaptation. These uncertainties will undoubtedly cause a future generation of program evaluators and library service professionals to decide to develop a new evaluation approach in response to changed circumstances.

Despite this note of caution, we emphasize that the process used in *Measuring Success* has enabled a concrete and compelling vision to emerge with a promise of helping library executives and administrators better address external policy-maker concerns for accountability and results and to better manage library programs in a continuing era of heightened public demand and scarce budgets.

Authors' Note

The views expressed are those of the authors and do not necessarily reflect the official position or policies of the Institute of Museum and Library Services.

Acknowledgments

The authors are grateful to their IMLS colleagues. They appreciate the reviews of various drafts of the chapter performed by Carlos Manjarrez, Mary Chute, Laurie Brooks, James Lonergan, Michele Farrell, and Timothy Owens for reviewing various drafts of the chapter. They especially thank Karen Motylewski for her high level of professionalism in engaging with her colleagues, leading to an improved argument through editing multiple versions of this chapter.

References

Boston, J., Martin, J., Pallot, J., & Walsh, P. (1996). *Public management: The New Zealand model*. Oxford, UK: Oxford University Press.
Bryson, J. B. (2004). *Strategic planning for public and nonprofit organizations: A guide to creating and sustaining organizations* (3rd ed.). San Francisco, CA: Jossey-Bass.

Farrior, M. (2005). *Breakthrough strategies for engaging the public: Emerging trends in communications and social science.* Retrieved from http://www.biodiverse.org/docs/publicationsandtipsheets/breakthroughstrategiesforengagingthepublic.pdf

Gladwell, M. (2000). *The tipping point: How little things can make a big difference.* New York, NY: Little Brown.

Harris, E. (2005). An introduction to theory of change. *Evaluation Exchange, XI*(2). Retrieved from http://www.hfrp.org/evaluation/the-evaluation-exchange/issue-archive/evaluation-methodology/an-introduction-to-theory-of-change

Heath, C., & Heath, D. (2007). *Made to stick: Why some ideas survive and others stick.* New York, NY: Random House.

Institute for Museum and Library Services. (2011). *Public libraries survey: Fiscal year 2009.* Retrieved from http://www.imls.gov/assets/1/News/PLS2009.pdf

LeFebvre, R. C. (2010). *On social marketing and social change: Selected readings 2005–2009* [Online, on-demand publication]. Createspace.

McDavid, J. C., & Huse, I. (2012). Legislator uses of public performance reports: Findings from a five year study. *American Journal of Evaluation, 33*(1), 7–25.

Patton, M. Q. (2008). *Utilization-focused evaluation* (4th ed.). Thousand Oaks, CA: Sage.

Patton, M. Q. (2011). *Developmental evaluation: Applying complexity concepts to enhance evaluation innovation and use.* New York, NY: Guilford Press.

Penual, W. R., Sussex, W., & Korbak, C. (2006). Investigating the potential of using social network analysis in educational evaluation. *American Journal of Evaluation, 27*(4), 437–451.

Rogers, E. I. (1962). *Diffusion of innovations.* New York, NY: Free Press.

Rogers, P. J. (2008). Using program theory for complicated and complex programme evaluation. *The International Journal of Theory, Research and Practice, 14*(1), 29–48. Retrieved from http://www.eval.org/search10/session.asp?sessionid=7437&presenterid=2099

Rogers, P. J. (2010, November). Representing simple, complicated and complex aspects in logics models for evaluation quality. Paper presented at the meeting of the American Evaluation Association, San Antonio, TX.

Rossi, P. H., Lipsey, M. W., & Freeman, H. E. (2004). *Evaluation: A systematic approach* (7th ed.). Thousand Oaks, CA: Sage.

Russ-Eft, D. F., & Preskill, H. S. (2009). *Evaluation in organizations: A systematic approach to enhancing learning, performance, and change* (2nd ed.). Philadelphia, PA: Basic Books.

Schelling, T. C. (1971). Dynamic models of segregation. *Journal of Mathematical Sociology, 1*(2), 143–186.

Schmitt, E. (2007, December 21). The theory of change primary. *The American Prospect.* Retrieved from http://prospect.org/article/tehory-change-primary

Weiss, C. H. (1972). *Evaluating action programs: Readings in social action and education.* Boston, MA: Allyn and Bacon.

Weiss, C. H. (1995). The four I's of school reform: How interests, ideology, information and institution affect teachers and principals. *Harvard Education Review, 65*(4), 571–593.

The New York State Library's Outcome-Based Evaluation Training Initiative: Using Training, Online Support, and Integration to Measure Impact

Amanda R. Latreille[a], Mary Ann Stiefvater[b] and Mary Linda Todd[b]
[a]AmaLat Consulting, Elbridge, NY, USA
[b]New York State Library, New York State Education Department, Albany, NY, USA

Abstract

The chapter describes the Outcome-Based Evaluation (OBE) Initiative of the New York State Library (NYSL) from its start in 2003. Through extensive training, online support, and integration into statewide processes and grant projects, the initiative has brought OBE to New York State's library community with the overall goals of measuring impact and leveraging funding. NYSL's OBE activities and lessons learned are especially helpful to those interested in developing a similar initiative or aspects of it. The activities and findings of the initiative are reviewed including implementation of the ten-stage OBE Training Plan that was the project's foundation. Logic models and outcomes were used to plan and evaluate most of the initiative.

The OBE Initiative has been a success on many levels. Training and support have been effective in teaching library staff how to implement OBE at regional and local levels. The approach has been widely accepted by libraries. NYSL has also integrated OBE techniques into several statewide processes and grant projects. Through OBE, libraries are able to determine the impact of their programs and services. Outcome data leads to improved planning and better decision making. Users ultimately receive higher quality library services, resulting in a more literate community and workforce. OBE can also support advocacy efforts, leading to increased funding for services. While many in the library community are now using OBE, very few have developed a statewide initiative. The chapter is original and has high value. Each of the three authors has carried out multiple aspects of the project.

Keywords: Outcomes evaluation; planning; training; impact; libraries; New York State

CONTEXTS FOR ASSESSMENT AND OUTCOME EVALUATION IN LIBRARIANSHIP
ADVANCES IN LIBRARIANSHIP, VOL. 35
© 2012 by Emerald Group Publishing Limited
ISSN: 0065-2830
DOI: 10.1108/S0065-2830(2012)0000035005

I. Introduction

The New York State Library (NYSL) launched an Outcome-Based Evaluation (OBE) Initiative in 2003, through a partnership with the federal Institute of Museum and Library Services (IMLS). At the time, IMLS was emerging as a leader in OBE. The federal agency was using the evaluation as the standard for reporting IMLS grant activities, in order to meet the requirements of the Government Performance and Results Act of 1993 (IMLS, 2011). In 2001, NYSL staff participated in OBE training hosted by IMLS staff in Washington, DC. The following year, an action plan was developed that would bring the evaluation approach to the library community in New York State.

Early on, NYSL saw great potential in OBE for planning and advocacy efforts. In 2001, library impact data was lacking at state, regional, and local levels. Many library systems and libraries were struggling with rising costs and stagnant funding levels. Some were facing budget cuts. The incidents on September 11, 2001 brought added uncertainty to the financial future of New York's libraries. Public safety and the war on terror were the nation's newest priorities. It was predicted that libraries would have to work even harder to compete for limited public funds. Additionally, other national agencies and organizations, such as the United Way, were already using OBE to demonstrate the value of their programs and services. Some private funders, such as the Bill & Melinda Gates Foundation, were requesting outcomes on grant applications and reports. Yet, the majority of library professionals in New York State lacked any formal knowledge of OBE. Most were completely inexperienced in its use.

For these reasons, NYSL developed a statewide OBE Initiative, which remains in place today. The initiative consists of three key components: (1) OBE training; (2) online OBE support and resources; and (3) integration of OBE into NYSL processes and grant projects. While the first two components began in 2003, the third developed over time. All three components and several lessons learned are discussed in detail in this chapter.

II. OBE Training

Training was the initial priority of Component 1 of the OBE Initiative. With the majority of library professionals lacking knowledge of this evaluation approach, NYSL saw OBE training as the critical first step to implementation. Prior to the project, most library staff in New York State were tracking only outputs, such as the number of programs and program attendants.

Library staff members were unfamiliar with outcomes and did not have the skills necessary to measure library impact and value. OBE had not been a part of their professional development.

In 2001, two Library Development Specialists, Sara McCain and Mary Linda Todd, participated in IMLS training and were designated as NYSL's OBE Team. In 2002, they developed a ten-stage OBE Training Plan that was later approved by IMLS (see below and Appendix A), and federal Library Service and Technology Act (LSTA) funds would be used to support the project. OBE training was already a component of NYSL's LSTA 2002–2007 Five-Year Plan (NYSL, 2011c).

The OBE Training Plan was intended to jump-start the broader OBE Initiative that currently exists. It applied a top-down approach to training, beginning with NYSL staff. Library systems would subsequently receive OBE instruction from NYSL, and then offer similar training to their member libraries. It was a train-the-trainer approach. In New York State, there are 73 library systems that serve and support more than 6500 public, school, and special libraries (NYSL, 2011d).

A. Training Plan

The following summarizes the OBE Training Plan as written in 2004:

- *Stage 1*: IMLS will offer an introductory OBE training for NYSL staff in Albany.
- *Stages 2 through 6*: The OBE Team will develop a comprehensive OBE training package. The package will be tested with library system staff, and an overall review of the training will follow. IMLS will provide advanced OBE training and technical assistance in finalizing the training package. The OBE Team will revise the training package and approve for use.
- *Stage 7*: NYSL will implement OBE throughout NYSL and library systems. OBE will be incorporated into all NYSL guidelines for plans, applications, and reports. OBE training for library system staff will be offered in multiple locations across New York State.
- *Stage 8*: NYSL will train instructors to teach OBE to member libraries (through library systems). A training template for their use will be developed to supplement the OBE training package.
- *Stages 9 and 10*: Library systems will develop training plans for implementing OBE in their member libraries. NYSL will review the plans and provide technical assistance in refining them. Library systems will then conduct OBE training for member libraries.

While some stages of the OBE Training Plan remain ongoing, the plan was generally carried out from 2003 to 2006. An evaluation consultant, Dr. Eleanor Carter, was hired by NYSL to work with the OBE Team. During *Stage 1*, NYSL staff, including the OBE Team, completed introductory OBE training conducted by IMLS in 2003. The 25 participants achieved the following two desired outcomes: (1) they understood OBE components and practiced building logic models; and (2) they wrote appropriate outcomes and indicators for at least one program they administer. Interestingly, the OBE Initiative itself was the first NYSL project to be planned and evaluated using OBE.

For *Stages 2 through 6*, a prototype of the training package was developed by the OBE Team. The package included a Power Point presentation, a training manual for participants, training activities, resource handouts, and a logic model framework. A journal template was also developed as a means of capturing feedback about the training package.

B. Prototype Testing and Revision

The prototype was tested during a two-day, pilot workshop for 15 library system staff members in May 2004. Participants completed a post-workshop survey and submitted a journal of their workshop experience. Overall, survey responses indicated that the vast majority of participants felt significantly more confident in implementing OBE. Each participant submitted complete and appropriate logic models demonstrating their ability to write outcomes, indicators, and other OBE elements. Each participant also indicated having no prior use of OBE. Their journals detailed a number of suggested improvements and changes to the training package.

After reviewing suggestions, the OBE Team made more than 40 revisions. These included further clarification of certain topics, tips for completing the more difficult training activities, more library-specific examples of outcomes and indicators, and an independent end-of-workshop exercise that could be used to evaluate individual learning. The latter was an important addition because the training was designed for teams of three to four library professionals to collaborate on one project. In some cases, teams were composed of individuals who had different job titles and responsibilities (although this was avoided if possible). While participants practiced developing a logic model as a team throughout the training, the last exercise would assess whether or not they could each write outcomes on their own. The revised Basic OBE Training Manual was finalized and approved in August 2004 (NYSL, 2011e).

C. Training Logic Model

Concurrently, the OBE Team finalized the OBE Training Logic Model (see below and Appendix B) that would assist in *Stage 7* of the OBE Training Plan and in evaluation of workshops. The document also served as an example for workshop participants, so they could see that NYSL was using OBE to evaluate statewide projects and not simply training others in its use.

Please note that another aspect of Stage 7, incorporating OBE into guidelines for NYSL plans, applications, and reports, is discussed in Component 3: Integration of OBE into NYSL Processes and Grant Projects.

The following is the OBE Training Logic Model, with actual results for each outcome:

- *Outcome 1 (immediate)*: Training participants plan OBE measures of intended program outcomes.
  - Indicator: Number and percent of training participants who write at least three clearly defined, measurable outcomes in an OBE plan (logic model) as assessed by a trained reviewer during the workshop and by a final independent exercise
  - Data source: Trained reviewer rating of all required elements of measurable outcomes
  - Data intervals: End of workshop
  - Target audience: All who complete the training ($N = 75$)
  - Target achievement level: 90% ($N = 68$ out of 75 participants)
  - Results: From 2004 to 2006, NYSL offered 13 two-day Basic OBE Workshops in various locations across New York State. A total of 155 participants, representing 60 library systems, completed the workshop. This was more than double the original target audience. Each participant was tested in their ability to write appropriate outcomes, indicators, and other OBE elements using the final independent exercise previously mentioned. All but one participant completed the exercise successfully for an achievement level of 99.4% (154 out of 155). That one participant wrote outputs instead of outcomes.

- *Outcome 2 (intermediate)*: Training participants use OBE in their LSTA grant applications.
  - Indicator: Number and percent of training participants who submit an LSTA grant application to NYSL during a subsequent LSTA grant cycle who achieve a normalized score of 90
  - Data source: Grant reviewer rating including inter-rater check to achieve normalized score
  - Data intervals: End of LSTA grant application review
  - Target audience: All who complete the training and also submit an LSTA grant application during a subsequent LSTA grant cycle
  - Target achievement level: 50% ($N = 37$ out of 75 participants)
  - Results: The indicator for this outcome ended up requiring revision. The original plan was to examine the reviewer ratings on LSTA grant applications submitted by library staff who completed OBE training and who subsequently submitted an acceptable application. This, however, did not prove to be a measure of whether or not OBE was a part of the approved proposal, as some applications that scored well were not appropriate for OBE. As an alternative, the OBE Team reviewed all 2005 and 2006 LSTA applications for the presence of OBE elements (a review of LSTA 2004 grants submitted prior to OBE training provided a baseline and showed no use of OBE). A total of 65 applications were submitted, but only 26 met the two qualifying criteria: (1) the individual submitting the proposal had completed OBE training; and (2) the proposal could be evaluated using OBE. The review showed that all 26 (or 100%) included multiple elements of OBE. Also to note, four LSTA applications included outcomes that reached the end user (patrons) in addition to library staff. During the training, library system participants were asked to write logic models that included the end user, even though their work at the system level primarily involves serving member libraries (their member library staff then serves the end user). As this is valuable impact data for planning and advocacy efforts, it was encouraging to see some applicants incorporating end user outcomes into their evaluation plans.

- *Outcome 3 (long term)*: Training participants use OBE in their LSTA grant reports to show measurable results of technology training programs (at the time, LSTA training program grant projects were, by far, the most popular type of grant project application).
  - Indicator: Number and percent of training participants who received an LSTA grant during a subsequent grant cycle who report results of intended outcomes as assessed by a trained NYSL reviewer
  - Data source: Trained NYSL reviewer rating
  - Data interval: End of LSTA grant report review
  - Target audience: All who complete the training and also received an LSTA grant during a subsequent grant cycle
  - Target achievement level: 90% ($N = 33$ out of 37 participants who achieved Outcome 2)
  - Results: Of the 26 applications that qualified for review, 17 (or 65.4%) reported on outcomes. Several others referred to outcomes, but impact data was not available at the time of the submitted reports. Some mixing of outcomes and outputs was also evident. In some cases, impact data was not clearly outlined using OBE elements, but had to be extracted from the narrative. Five reports were clear in their use of OBE, and could have been considered model reports.

- *Outcome 4 (long term)*: Training participants report that follow-up mentoring helped them to better apply OBE.
  - Indicator: Number and percent of training participants who use follow-up mentoring who score 80 or better on a 100-point evaluation scale.
  - Data source: Satisfaction survey
  - Data interval: After six months of mentoring service, then annually
  - Target audience: All training participants who request follow-up mentoring
  - Target achievement level: 90% of participants who use the service
  - Results: As of 2006 when the OBE Training Logic Model was evaluated, a formal mentoring service was not in place (see Outcome 5 below). The evaluation consultant who conducted the OBE training and NYSL staff provided hours of informal mentoring via phone and e-mail. There were multiple cases of participants e-mailing draft logic models, grant applications, and data collection instruments to the OBE Team for review and technical assistance. As these were informal interactions on an as needed basis, the individuals were not surveyed.

Overall, the results of the OBE Training Logic Model evaluation indicated that NYSL had made great strides in training library system staff. The OBE training package was a proven success, but there was still a great deal of work to do to support statewide implementation of OBE. Evaluation indicated that many participants wanted advanced training in OBE. Many participants wrote outcomes during the Basic OBE Workshops that required data collection instruments which they were unable to develop. Many participants lacked the knowledge to report outcomes or merge outcome and output data in a report, as seen with Outcome 3. Therefore, instead of offering the formal mentoring service described in Outcome 4, the OBE Team decided it would be more effective to offer Advanced OBE Workshops to those who had successfully completed basic training.

D. Advanced Training and Train-the-Trainer

The following outcome with indicators was written prior to the additional advanced training. Actual results are included:

- *Outcome 5 (immediate)*: Participants apply OBE techniques to individualized projects meeting standards for collecting outcomes.
  - Indicator 1: Number and percent of participants who complete at least one acceptable OBE product as assessed by trained observers during the workshop
  - Indicator 2: Number and percent of participants who complete at least one acceptable OBE product as assessed by participant self-report at the end of the workshop
  - Results: In 2005 and 2006, two sessions of Advanced OBE Workshops were held for a total of 21 participants, mostly library system staff. Participants were asked to bring a completed logic model to the training that required some form of advanced work. During the workshops, participants developed data collection instruments, such as checklists, rubrics, and surveys, analyzed outcome and output data, and developed reports. Participants were expected to complete the workshop with one usable OBE product in hand. This was achieved. All 21 participants (or 100%) were successful in meeting both indicators. The majority developed multiple products for use with their individual logic models.

While the evaluation of the OBE Training Logic Model was being completed, the OBE Team moved to implementing the final stages of the OBE Training Plan. Originally, NYSL was to train instructors and create a training template, and then in turn, these instructors through library systems would train member library staff (a train-the-trainer approach). However, *Stages 8 through 10* did not occur exactly as planned. Several variables led to different actions and a mix of solutions to bring training to member libraries. This work continues to be an ongoing part of the OBE Initiative today.

Back in 2005, some library systems indicated that they were not prepared to offer Basic OBE Workshops. Some had not sent the staff members who would be their instructors to basic training when it was offered by NYSL. While many had some experience using OBE with system projects, they had not yet worked through the training package as a participant. Other staff who had attended basic training felt they were novices, not experts in OBE. The participants did not feel the initial two days of training had equipped them to teach others.

The OBE Team, therefore, decided to carry out a variety of activities to address these issues. First, a two-day Train-the-Trainer OBE Workshop, conducted by the evaluation consultant, was held in October 2005. In preparation, the OBE Team developed a comprehensive Train-the-Trainer OBE Manual (NYSL, 2011e). The manual included commentary for each of the slides in the Basic OBE Training Manual, exercises to practice identifying and addressing OBE problems and questions, and sample data collection instruments. Ten participants completed the training and were certified by NYSL as OBE trainers. Each participant was tested on a final independent exercise that included samples of typical errors made by OBE learners. All 10 (or 100%) demonstrated the ability to identify the problems and propose solutions in a manner similar to what would be required of an OBE trainer. These 10 participants had now completed Basic, Advanced, and Train-the-Trainer OBE Workshops, for a total of six days of OBE training. Many have since gone on to offer OBE workshops. One Certified OBE Trainer, for example, has trained approximately 200 library professionals to date, the majority being library staff in New York.

NYSL also continued to offer two-day Basic and Advanced OBE Workshops. Registration was expanded to include member library staff in 2007 (previously it was only available to library system staff). From 2007 to 2010, multiple workshops were conducted by evaluation consultants, supported by LSTA funds. OBE training remains a part of the NYSL's current LSTA 2007–2012 Five-Year Plan (NYSL, 2011c).

E. Training Through Grant Projects

OBE training was also incorporated into grant projects whenever possible. If NYSL would be reporting project outcomes, training was included in grant proposal activities. This became an effective means of covering the costs necessary in providing library systems and member libraries with OBE training, and ultimately, in helping participants obtain valuable impact data.

The following are five examples of NYSL grant projects that contained OBE training (2005–2011):

- *Staying Connected*: NYSL partnered with the Bill & Melinda Gates Foundation from 2004 to 2008 in both Phase 1 and Phase 2 of the Staying Connected Grant Program. The project's purpose was to support public access computing in public libraries through hardware upgrades, Internet connectivity, and training and technical support. NYSL participated in the hardware upgrades and training support components. Libraries that chose to participate in the training component could select to participate in OBE training sessions. A consultant was hired by NYSL to conduct these sessions, and as a result, 327 library staff members gained a basic knowledge of OBE techniques. They demonstrated their new OBE skills through planning technology training sessions and other programs (NYSL, 2008a, 2009a).

- *Making It REAL*: In 2004, IMLS approved NYSL's grant proposal for a statewide recruitment project, titled "Making It REAL! Recruitment, Education, and Learning: Creating a New Generation of Librarians to Serve All New Yorkers." The three-year project funded the recruitment of 41 library school students through 19 project partners, which included 12 library systems, 6 graduate schools of library and information science, and the New York Library Association. The concept of Teaching Libraries was introduced. The grant proposal included OBE activities, and a consultant was hired to carry out this work. Each of the 19 project partners were required to create their own OBE logic models following a joint meeting and training, held at the project's start. The evaluation consultant regularly worked with each partner to develop and complete the logic models throughout the grant period (NYSL, 2009c).

- *Rural Library Sustainability*: NYSL partnered with WebJunction and the Bill & Melinda Gates Foundation on the Rural Library Sustainability Grant Program from 2005 to 2007. The project supported public libraries serving fewer than 25,000 people by training participants in implementing community-specific action plans to sustain their public access computing services and library programming. While the project contained a specific curriculum, NYSL developed outcomes for project management and also added training components that included OBE. In 2006, ten daylong workshops were held in multiple regions of the state. Following the workshops, participants applied the skills learned to develop a customized action plan to actively sustain computing services and programming in their libraries. By project completion, 525 participants (or 98%) had created action plans, and 455 (or 85%) reported implementing an activity from the plan. In addition, all 535 participants, staff from library systems and libraries, received some exposure to OBE and its value in measuring impact (NYSL, 2009b).

- *EqualAccess Libraries*: The result of a partnership between NYSL and Libraries for the Future, New York EqualAccess Libraries brought comprehensive training and support in outreach, collaboration, and advocacy to public library staff in New York State. A total of 99 individuals participated from 2005 to 2008. Part of the training involved developing work plans and writing outcomes to measure the impact of programs and services, primarily for three specific target audiences: (1) adolescents (Youth Access); (2) retirees (Lifelong Access); and (3) health consumers (Health Access). The NYSL-developed Basic OBE Training Manual was used to create a condensed OBE curriculum for the project. Outcomes were developed to measure the effectiveness of the training workshops. The vast majority of participants reported increased confidence in applying the skills covered in the training via online surveys. Some workshop participants reported using outcomes in grant applications and advocacy efforts post-training (NYSL, 2008b).

- *Broadbandexpress@yourlibrary*: In 2010, the Broadbandexpress@yourlibrary Grant Program was launched by NYSL through a partnership with the National Telecommunications and Information Administration (NTIA). This project is responsible for developing Public Computing Centers (PCCs) and Teleconferencing Centers in 30 libraries located within economically distressed communities, and five E-Mobile Computing Training Units in rural and underserved areas. Higher level outcomes were included in the original grant application to NTIA, and NYSL subsequently added project management outcomes for participating libraries and OBE training into the grant activities. The first workshop occurred in 2010. Participants were introduced to OBE concepts, and given time to brainstorm preliminary project outcomes for their PCC or E-Mobile Unit. The next training, held in early 2011, was a two-day concentrated workshop on evaluation and sustainability. OBE was covered by an evaluation consultant, with the Basic OBE Training Manual serving as the foundation. Workshop materials were customized for the project, and detailed outcome examples included. Participants from the 35 PCCs and E-Mobile Units were required to submit OBE plans and data collection instruments for review by NYSL staff. The expectation is that sub-recipient course offerings and management decisions will be made in light of these plans, particularly since interim OBE reports will be submitted at six-month intervals for review. While Broadbandexpress@yourlibary is not yet complete, training materials and participant OBE plans are available on the NYSL web site (2011f).

F. Lessons Learned

Provide adequate training time, especially for practice and questions. For close to a decade, NYSL has offered two-day Basic OBE Workshops. During those two days, the entire time has consistently been used by training participants. Rarely do library professionals get hours of uninterrupted time, especially for planning and evaluation. Most participants take full advantage of the opportunity to work with others as a team and brainstorm outcomes and indicators. This also gives the trainer ample time to move from team to team, answering questions and providing feedback. It is important to note that OBE does not come easy for many individuals. It is a new way of thinking about evaluation. While participants know their work has impact and value, specifically identifying and measuring it using outcomes can be challenging. Providing plenty of time and a non-rushed training environment can help foster OBE learning. If OBE must be covered in a much shorter time period, the training curriculum should be introductory in nature and cover only the basics of writing outcomes, as not to overwhelm participants.

Encourage the use of meaningful examples and actual participant projects. Basic OBE Workshops should include several team exercises. Participants of similar job titles and responsibilities should be grouped together whenever possible. For example, public librarians may make up one team, and school librarians may make up another. They are then encouraged to select a team project that is meaningful to everyone in the group. If the project is something they may actually implement in their work and understand, then it is more likely they will be able to write appropriate outcomes and indicators. For example, a group of public librarians responsible for youth services may draft a logic model for a summer reading program, a common activity of public libraries. If possible, the trainer can also request that participants submit project ideas prior to the training and assign teams in advance. This can be very effective, as the trainer can also weed out any projects that are not a good match for OBE. Lastly, the final independent exercise in basic training should be an individual's actual project, whether in existence or planned. The participant then leaves with a real-world example in hand, ready for implementation.

Incorporate data collection instruments into every training. As mentioned earlier, the OBE Team learned that having participants develop logic models was often not enough. If OBE was to be fully implemented, participants needed assistance in developing data collection instruments that specifically measured outcomes. For example, many participants had no experience in creating checklists, rubrics, and surveys. NYSL offered Advanced OBE Workshops to meet this need, but every workshop, even introductory training, should include examples and a list of references for more information. There are several how-to guides and tips online, especially for developing surveys.

Offer post-training assistance and mentoring. Again, many training participants find OBE concepts difficult to understand. Some grasp the evaluation approach right away, while others need time and repeated exposure before understanding the concept. That is why offering post-training assistance is essential. NYSL has continued to provide informal mentoring to participants since holding its first OBE training in 2004. Often individuals will work on logic models, grant applications, or data collection instruments after training, and questions arise. Others have project-specific concerns that they would rather discuss one-on-one, versus in a group setting. This service has been effective and appreciated by participants.

III. Online OBE Support and Resources

In Component 2, the OBE Team developed a web site in 2005 housed within the NYSL web site (2011a). Its primary purpose is to provide online support and resources to training participants and independent OBE learners. Post-workshop, the web site is a place where participants can turn for further assistance, whether it is a day, a month, or a year or more after training. The contents of the web site are highlighted at each workshop. Other library professionals, unfamiliar with OBE but in need of outcomes for grant writing or reporting, can also visit the site for information and instruction. As a secondary purpose, the NYSL uses the site as a means for sharing the OBE Initiative with other state library agencies or library systems interested in rolling out a similar initiative or an aspect of it.

The major elements of the OBE web site are:

- *Training manuals*: Two manuals, the Basic OBE Training Manual and the Train-the-Trainer OBE Manual can be freely downloaded from the web site.
- *Best practices*: The site includes links to model OBE grant applications, organized into three categories: (1) applications illustrating the use of a complete OBE package, including a logic model; (2) applications illustrating measurements; and (3) applications illustrating qualitative results.
- *Introductory webinar*: Added in 2010, the webinar provides users with an introduction to OBE concepts. The 20-minute session covers the basics of writing outcomes using real-world examples. It is intended for those who are new to OBE or in need of a refresher (NYSL, 2010a).
- *Resource links*: The site includes links to several other OBE resources, including the IMLS and United Way web sites and other states library OBE pages.
- *Certified trainers*: As mentioned earlier, NYSL trained 10 OBE trainers in 2005. These individuals are listed and may be contacted for OBE training.

• *Initiative information*: The site houses the OBE Training Plan and the OBE Training Logic Model. The training results discussed under Component 1 are also included, as well as an ongoing, bulleted list of NYSL OBE activities, from 2003 to present.

A. Lessons Learned

Provide organized, easy to navigate, and current online information. As with any web site, design is key. The OBE Team purposely selected a simple organizational and navigational scheme for its OBE web site, in keeping with the style of the broader NYSL site. OBE news and updates are highlighted at the top of the homepage, and are kept current. Links to web site elements are clearly visible. Nothing turns users away like outdated information, such as old training workshop dates, or broken links. Regular review of the site is essential. In addition, contact information for assistance from staff should be included, since users sometimes need individual assistance beyond the capabilities of online resources.

Offer varied formats to meet diverse user needs. NYSL is continuing to explore different formats for online OBE instruction. Currently, the training manuals and the introductory webinar are offered on the web site. Users may need the detailed information and examples found in the manuals, or they may simply want to review basic concepts via the webinar. Also, some users learn better and retain more through guided audio/visual presentations. Use of the webinar is growing and had been viewed almost 4000 times from mid-2010 to the end of 2011. Linking to other OBE resources can also supplement the formats offered.

Promote online resources regularly. NYSL promotes the OBE web site through a variety of communication channels, including meetings, conferences, trainings, newsletters, and listservs. In addition, links to the online resources are included in grant application instructions and guidelines. Each time NYSL begins a new project utilizing OBE, it becomes an opportunity to educate others about the approach and direct them to the web site.

IV. Integration of OBE into NYSL Processes and Grant Projects

With training and online support in place, Component 3 became possible, integrating OBE concepts into NYSL processes and grant projects. OBE would become the new evaluation standard. NYSL has never viewed OBE as a passing trend, and this attitude was conveyed repeatedly to staff and the library community. By the time integration had begun, NYSL and library system staff members were beginning to fully understand and accept OBE. The introduction of outcomes into statewide initiatives was the logical next step. The OBE Team served as experts and reviewers for integrating OBE into internal processes and projects managed by other NYSL staff.

At the state level, NYSL has experienced many of the same OBE benefits of those at regional and local levels. Statewide integration has contributed toward planning, decision making, and the allocation of resources. Improvements in program and service design have resulted, ultimately leading to higher quality services for library systems, member libraries, and their staff and users. Common program indicators have been identified for use in multiple projects, boosting overall efficiency. Impact data has also been essential in explaining the value of New York State's libraries to policy makers and funders.

The following are three examples of OBE integration into NYSL processes:

- *LSTA Five-Year Plan*: NYSL receives federal LSTA funds each year, distributed by IMLS. To receive the funds, state library agencies are required to develop a five-year plan detailing how the funds will be used. IMLS reviews and approves the plan. NYSL's current LSTA 2007–2012 Five-Year Plan is organized similar to an OBE logic model. The document contains a needs section, goals, activities, outputs, and outcomes. The target outputs and outcomes are used to measure the effectiveness of the plan's activities annually and through a complete evaluation every five years. The data is also used to guide the development of the future plan (NYSL, 2011c).
- *NYSL LSTA Grant Programs*: Since 2005, NYSL has incorporated OBE evaluation techniques into the LSTA grant programs offered to New York State's library systems. Applicants are requested to indicate they have done a needs assessment, describe project goals, and explain what evaluation methods will be used. They are expected to not only report outputs, but also at least two outcomes. Best practices of LSTA grant reporting are available on NYSL's OBE web site (NYSL, 2011a).
- *Library System Plans of Service*: Each of the 73 library systems in New York State must have an approved Five-Year Plan of Service. The document identifies, organizes, and provides an overview of the library system's service program, including intended changes in services or priorities. The plan emphasizes what the library system proposes to accomplish and whom the library system serves. Since 2006, elements of the plan have resembled those of a logic model. Goals must be articulated, a needs assessment must be demonstrated, and there is also an evaluation component. Systems must detail their evaluation approach and include user satisfaction data collection and analysis (NYSL, 2011b).

Since 2004, NYSL has also integrated OBE into all relevant statewide grant projects. Many of the NYSL grant projects that incorporated OBE concepts (and specifically training) were previously described under Component 1: OBE Training of this chapter. There is one project, however, that has not yet been discussed, and utilized outcome data to show great impact on public libraries, communities, and users in New York State.

This project, titled the Opportunity Online Hardware Grant Program, was funded by the Bill & Melinda Gates Foundation. It began in 2007 and was completed in 2010.

The program was developed to help upgrade public access computing services in libraries that serve high-need communities and were struggling to keep pace with advancements in technology. Grants were given to 421 of New York's public libraries for the purchase of new hardware for public use. In addition, the program, through technology planning and advocacy training, aimed to help libraries secure funding to sustain hardware upgrades over time. Participation in this grant was based on two criteria: (1) percent of the population living at or below the poverty level; and (2) computer and Internet services that were demonstrably in danger of becoming obsolete.

The original grant application submitted to the Bill & Melinda Gates Foundation included OBE elements. The proposal indicated that 421 (or 100%) of participating libraries would utilize TechAtlas, an online hardware inventory tool. Also, the majority (at least 55%) would report permanent technology line items in subsequent budgets. Using OBE and developing these targets set the application apart from other states' proposals, and resulted in a grant allocation that enabled NYSL to offer more training. Ultimately, libraries learned to highlight user outcomes, such as public utilization of computers for work, recreation, learning, medical information, and e-government services, and to ask their boards and public for a permanent technology line item in their budget.

The project's evaluation plan was further developed with three key outcomes that built upon the original targets. These are listed below, and explored in detail in the impact report, *Opportunity Online Hardware Grant: Providing Opportunities Through Public Access Computing* (NYSL, 2010b):

- *Outcome 1*: Participating libraries improve their technology planning and services.
- *Outcome 2*: Participating libraries increase use of their technology services and attract new patrons.
- *Outcome 3*: Participating libraries successfully advocate for new funding for technology and build support from new and existing partners.

Project findings from participant surveys, reports, and interviews indicated that the first and second outcomes were achieved in the majority to vast majority of participating libraries (completed surveys were received from 92% of the 421 libraries). For the third outcome, 45% of survey respondents reported that the grant program assisted the library in advocating for new funding for technology. An impressive 34% of respondents reported that their library obtained new ongoing funding for technology. Not only were these libraries able to secure the matching funds, but they were so successful in their advocacy efforts that local policymakers saw the need to commit long-term funding for hardware upgrades and maintenance. Additionally, 41% felt the program helped the library build upon and strengthen existing partnerships, while 32% felt the program helped in establishing new partnerships. The impact report includes numerous participant examples illustrating the program's key outcomes, as well as project challenges identified through OBE analysis. The outcome data ultimately provided a clear picture of the project's value and areas for future improvement.

A. Lessons Learned

Use OBE for project planning from the start. OBE is both a planning and evaluation tool. NYSL has learned that it is most effective when used to shape a project from the beginning stages. Trying to develop outcomes half way through or at the end of a project simply does not work. This defeats the purpose of designing a project to specifically meet a need and achieve the desired outcomes. However, there should be flexibility built into an OBE logic model, as unintentional outcomes do arise. This unexpected information can be just as valuable in measuring the effectiveness of programs and services.

Set grant proposals apart with outcomes and training. NYSL has been successful in receiving multiple grant awards in recent years. A primary reason is the inclusion of OBE elements in grant applications and proposals. When project outcomes are outlined, funders can clearly see how their grant monies will specifically benefit the target audience. It puts the emphasis on the impact, not the activities themselves. In this age of accountability and responsible spending, this is information they need. Adding OBE training to grant activities shows funders that the support will be in place to carry out this work, and that the applicant has fully thought the project and its evaluation component through. NYSL is winning grant awards because proposals demonstrate and build upon the impact of previous statewide projects, thereby leveraging funding opportunities.

Measure the impact on end users, whenever possible. OBE is used at its best when end user outcomes are measured, determining the impact of programs and services on communities. This has been a challenge at times simply because NYSL often works with library systems on projects that in turn must work with member libraries to obtain this data. With many library systems and libraries in New York State struggling with budget constraints and fewer staff, it can be difficult to carry out these tasks from the state level down. That said, NYSL continues to explore ways in which user outcomes can be measured. This information can also be especially meaningful to funders and policymakers.

Write outcomes for multiple purposes. When writing project outcomes, NYSL has consistently considered all stakeholders. For instance, outcomes of value to funders, outcomes that will lead to the improvement of library system programs and services, and outcomes that result in the development of local libraries are all explored. Many overlap, but it is important to be clear and deliberate from the start, and to think about future uses beyond the immediate project.

Use OBE with appropriate projects. OBE does not work for every project. It is best suited for projects in which a change occurs in the target audience, whether it is a change in knowledge, skills, attitude, or behavior. The change must be predicted and measurable. For example, NYSL has used OBE to measure the effectiveness of staff training on multiple occasions, as described previously in the chapter.

Develop an overall standard. Through the OBE Initiative, NYSL has developed a standard. NYSL staff members have been trained in OBE, know its value, and are encouraged to use it where appropriate. With a standard training curriculum also in place and trainers available, workshops can be rolled out as needed at regional and local levels. Training can easily be incorporated into grant proposals. NYSL no longer has to reinvent the wheel. The groundwork has been done, and NYSL's OBE materials are available online for others to utilize and share.

V. Conclusion

NYSL, since beginning the statewide OBE Initiative in 2003, has managed to train hundreds of library staff across New York State and provide continuous online support. NYSL has successfully integrated OBE techniques into both its internal processes and grant projects. Besides staff time, NYSL has spent a relatively small amount of funds in carrying out this initiative, leveraging grant funding to pay for the majority of the OBE training. As a result of these efforts, many library staff members have become skilled in using OBE techniques and are currently using the approach for project evaluation. Once viewed by some in the library community as a passing trend, OBE is now widely accepted. With New York's libraries still facing financial hardship with no end in sight, NYSL sees OBE as an ongoing tool for planning and advocacy efforts. NYSL plans to continue the work of the OBE Initiative to support libraries in demonstrating their strong value and relevance in today's world.

Acknowledgments

The authors would like to acknowledge the assistance of Dr. Eleanor Carter, the Institute of Museum and Library Services, and Sara McCain.

Appendix A: OBE Training Plan

For details on OBE Training Plan, see http://www.nysl.nysed.gov/libdev/obe/trn_plan.htm

Appendix B: OBE Training Logic Model

For details on OBE Training Logic Model, see http://www.nysl.nysed.gov/libdev/lsta/eval/obe/report.htm

References

Institute of Museum and Library Services. (2011). *Grant applicants/Outcome-based evaluation*. Retrieved from http://www.imls.gov/applicants/outcome_based_evaluations.aspx

New York State Library. (2008a). *Final Report for Staying Connected II Grant Program*. Retrieved from www.nysl.nysed.gov/libdev/gateslib/sc2/finalrep.htm

New York State Library and Libraries for the Future. (2008b). *Training and support in developing community responsive programming and services in public libraries—New York EqualAccess Libraries 2005–2008 Report*. Retrieved from http://www.nysl.nysed.gov/libdev/ea/0508rept.pdf

New York State Library. (2009a). *Staying Connected 1*. Retrieved from http://www.nysl.nysed.gov/libdev/gateslib/sc01.htm

New York State Library. (2009b). *Rural Library Sustainability Project/Partnering with the Gates Foundation and WebJunction*. Retrieved from http://www.nysl.nysed.gov/libdev/gateslib/rural.htm

New York State Library. (2009c). *Making it REAL! Recruitment, education, and learning: Creating a new generation of librarians to serve all New Yorkers*. Retrieved from http://www.nysl.nysed.gov/libdev/imls/index.html

New York State Library. (2010a). *Presentation: Basic outcome-based (OBE) evaluation webinar*. Retrieved from http://www.nysl.nysed.gov/libdev/obe/webinar/obepresentation.htm

New York State Library. (2010b). *Impact Report 2010: Opportunity Online Hardware Grant Program—Providing opportunities through public access computing*. Retrieved from http://www.nysl.nysed.gov/libdev/gateslib/hardware/impactreport.pdf

New York State Library. (2011a). *Outcome-based evaluation*. Retrieved from http://www.nysl.nysed.gov/libdev/obe/index.html

New York State Library. (2011b). *Library systems plans of service*. Retrieved from http://www.nysl.nysed.gov/libdev/pos/index.html

New York State Library. (2011c). *Library services and technology (LSTA) program in New York State*. Retrieved from http://www.nysl.nysed.gov/libdev/lsta/index.html
New York State Library. (2011d). *Annual report for public and association libraries— 2010*. Retrieved from http://www.nysl.nysed.gov/libdev/libs/index.html#annrep
New York State Library. (2011e). *Basic OBE training manual and train-the-trainer manual*. Retrieved from http://www.nysl.nysed.gov/libdev/obe/training.htm
New York State Library. (2011f). *Broadbandexpress@yourlibrary*. Retrieved from http://www.nysl.nysed.gov/libdev/nybbexpress/index.html

Documenting the Results of Good Intentions: Applying Outcomes Evaluation to Library Services for Children

Virginia A. Walter
Information Studies Department, University of California,
Los Angeles, CA, USA

Abstract

This chapter documents the evolution of the application of evaluation methods to public library services for children and teens in the United States. It describes the development of age-specific output measures and the subsequent requirement by funding agencies for outcome evaluations that measure changes in skills, attitudes, behavior, knowledge, or status as a result of an individual's participation in a service or program. Some early outcomes research studies are cited, and California initiative to implement statewide outcome evaluation of its Summer Reading Program is presented as a case study. Training and education are suggested as ways to counter the major challenges for wider implementation of outcome evaluation of youth services programs in public libraries.

Keywords: Public libraries; library services for children; library services for young adults; summer reading programs; outcomes evaluation

I. Introduction

For many librarians charged with the management of library services to children, interest in evaluation issues started with the publication of *Planning and Role Setting for Public Libraries: A Manual of Options and Procedures* by McClure, Owen, Zweizig, Lynch, and Van House (1987). This much-anticipated guide to strategic planning in public libraries, produced under the auspices of the Public Library Association, proposed that librarians engage in systematic community analysis efforts and then select the roles

© 2012 by Emerald Group Publishing Limited
ISSN: 0065-2830
DOI: 10.1108/S0065-2830(2012)0000035006
47

that would be the best fit between community needs and a library's mission
and resources. The eight roles were given by McClure *et al.* were:

- Community Activities Center,
- Community Information Center,
- Formal Education Support Center,
- Independent Learning Center,
- Popular Materials Library,
- Preschoolers' Door to Learning,
- Reference Library, and
- Research Center.

A companion volume, *Output Measures for Public Libraries* (Van House, Lynch,
McClure, Zweizig, & Rodger, 1987) proposed methods for quantifying the
library services that were implemented in response to the role-setting process.

Children's library services managers and advocates found these planning
and evaluation tools to be flawed in their failure to take into account the full
range of services, programs, and activities offered to children of all ages in
public libraries. The menu of roles above seemed to suggest that library
services to children were limited to preschool children. Clara Bohrer and
Kathleen Reif approached both the Public Library Association (PLA) and
the Association of Library Services to Children (ALSC) and persuaded
these two divisions of the American Library Association (ALA) to apply for a
grant from the US Department of Education, Library Research and Demonstration Program to develop and field test both quantitative and qualitative
evaluation measures for public library services to children under the age
of 14 and their caregivers. The resulting publication, *Output Measures for
Public Library Services to Children: A Manual of Standardized Procedures* (Walter,
1992), was the first effort to provide a national audience of children's
librarians and library directors with tools for both evaluating their full range
of services and communicating the results to various stakeholders. The
federal agency responsible for funding that effort was sufficiently impressed
that it asked the Young Adult Library Services Association (YALSA) to
submit a proposal for the development of similar evaluation techniques for
that aspect of library services. That grant produced another manual, *Output
Measures and More: Planning and Evaluating Public Library Services for Young
Adults* (Walter, 1995). Work on those two manuals, involving extensive field
testing and feedback from youth services librarians and public library
administrators, helped to make evaluation a more commonly accepted aspect
of managing library services to children and teens.

This chapter examines the next stage in evaluating children's and young
adult services in public libraries: the search for methods that would produce

evidence of the outcomes of library services for children. It provides an overview of several evaluation studies of children's and young adult services that were done using outcomes measures and looks in some detail at California's statewide initiative to apply outcomes evaluation to its Summer Reading Program.

II. The Rationale for Outcome Evaluation

A. Output Measures

Output measures, as set forth in the various manuals developed under the Public Library Development Program of PLA, were designed to enable librarians to quantify and document the work they did. They counted how many reference questions were answered or how many toddlers attended story time, or how many children attended story time. They made these statistics more meaningful by adding per capita measures. A small public library, for example, might report an "annual library visits by children" count of 5000. This statistic acquires more salience when compared with the number of children in the library's service area. If there were 1000 children in the service area, the output measure "children's library visits per child" is calculated to be 5 indicating, on average, every child in that community visited the library 5 times.

Not every public library implemented the use of the PLA planning process or output measures. However, the basic concepts involved in this approach to evaluation were widely disseminated through workshops sponsored by state libraries and programs at various library conferences. The next round of planning manuals from the PLA involved the publication of three editions of *Planning for Results* (Himmel & Wilson, 1998; Nelson, 2001, 2008). The biggest conceptual shift in the "planning for results" approach was in expansion of the library roles identified by McClure *et al.* (1987) to a menu of 14 Service Responses, which included 2 for youth services:

- Create Young Readers: Early Literacy, and
- Succeed in School: Homework Help.

Although PLA has published a number of companion volumes to the basic planning manuals, these have focused on issues such as managing and marketing rather than evaluating. Youth services librarians whose organizations have chosen to adopt this planning process have evidently chosen to work within the framework of the designated service responses. There has been no organized initiative to create a "planning for results for youth services."

B. Questioning Output Measures

Just when public librarians were becoming comfortable with the rationale and methodology for using output measures to quantify their services, funding agencies began to ask for the answers to a new question: what difference did it make? Five thousand children visited your library last year. So what? One thousand children attended preschool story hour. So what? What difference did it make in these children's behavior, attitudes, knowledge, or status because of the library's intervention? In other words, what were the desired outcomes of the library activity? Were those outcomes reached?

C. The Shift to Outcomes Measures

The Institute of Museum and Library Services (IMLS) replaced the Department of Education as the primary source of federal funds to libraries for demonstration projects. In the late 1990s, it began to require that grant proposals specify the desired outcomes of their projects and to budget for an evaluation of those outcomes. They even offered workshops for grant recipients to learn more about methods for evaluating outcomes, and a new term entered the vocabulary of children's librarians seeking federal grants: the logic model.

The outcomes logic model is a systems approach to evaluation. It asks the librarian to first consider the mission of the library and the considerations of various "influences" including funding agencies or potential program partners. The program purpose should be derived from those considerations and should be specific about what the library intends to do, for whom, and for what outcome or benefit. The outcome is presumed to be a change in skill, attitude, behavior, or status as a result on the participants as a result of the library's program. The program purpose in turn determines the inputs (resources needed to implement the program), activities designed to achieve the program outcomes, outputs (quantitative measures of those activities), and the outcomes themselves. Program planners are further instructed to identify the indicators that would provide data about observable behaviors and conditions, sources for those data, intervals at which data would be collected, and the targeted amount of desired change.

Clearly, implementing outcome evaluation was going to be a more complex and sophisticated process than even the most challenging output measures. Given minimal training and sufficient motivation, any librarian could collect the data needed for any of the earlier output measures and do the calculations required to analyze and understand the results. Outcome evaluations presented new challenges. In a survey of 139 California libraries conducted in 2010, respondents described outcome evaluation as a complicated undertaking with many barriers to implementation, including lack of resources and expertise (Sweeney, 2010).

It was not always easy for staff to identify the desired change in patrons' behaviors, attitudes, knowledge, or skills as a result of their participation in a library program. What did we really hope that toddlers would learn or do differently after they attended a series of storytimes? And if we knew the answer to that question, what would be the indicators of those changes? The indicators would almost always need to come from the patrons themselves, and librarians were professionally trained not to pry into the uses that library users made of the books they read or the answers they received in response to their reference questions. Dare we risk invading patron privacy by asking about how participation in a library service changed them? And of course, when the patrons were children, there were additional issues of parental consent and developmental concerns.

And yet, children's librarians recognized the value of knowing the outcomes of their work. They had long recognized that good intentions were not enough. In their hearts, they knew that storytimes and summer reading programs benefited children in many ways, but were hard-pressed to prove it. They knew that in more stringent budget situations, programs and activities without documented outcomes might be eliminated. So children's librarians began to get on board the "outcomes evaluation express." It is likely that many children's librarians used the training provided by IMLS and applied the logic model to their grant-funded projects, or hired professional evaluators to do the work for them. Unfortunately, the results of those efforts were usually not reported in the library press; and the knowledge gained was confined to local library jurisdictions.

III. Pioneering Outcome Evaluations of Library Services to Children and Teens

In spite of the methodological challenges presented by outcome evaluation, a few pioneering studies were conducted and their findings disseminated to a relatively broad audience.

In 2000 Cindy Mediavilla and Virginia Walter received an ALA Research Grant to develop a model for evaluating the outcomes of library homework assistance programs. As a conceptual framework, they used the six outcomes of positive youth development that were synthesized and articulated by the Public Libraries as Partners in Youth Development project:

- Youth contribute to their community.
- They feel safe in their environment.
- They have meaningful relationships with adults and peers.
- They achieve educational success.
- They develop marketable skills.
- They develop personal and social skills (Meyers, 2002).

The researchers used a mixed method approach to collect data from teens, library staff, and parents in seven libraries throughout the country. They were interested in teasing out outcomes for two different types of participation in homework assistance programs: those for teens who used the homework centers as students; and those who worked as volunteers or paid staff in the centers.

The results from the pilot study showed that homework centers contributed to positive youth development outcomes in a number of ways. For example, teens felt that they were contributing to their community whether they received homework assistance or helped to provide it. In the first instance, they said that by being good students they had a positive impact on their communities. Parents took a broader view, pointing out that students who used the homework centers were positive role models for their peers. Students who worked in library homework centers welcomed the opportunity to help other teens succeed. Those who lived in low-income communities had a particularly keen sense of giving back to their neighborhoods. For the most part, teens felt safe studying or working in the library after school. Some teens articulated a feeling of security that transcended safety from physical dangers. They felt comfortable and cared for by library staff. Everyone involved with the library homework centers saw them as places to learn skills that will someday be useful in the workplace. This went beyond obvious outcomes such as learning math and computer skills. Parents, teachers, and library staff noted that teens learned cooperation, discipline, courtesy, and problem-solving in the homework center environment. Teens with few employment opportunities in their communities found that working or volunteering in the homework programs gave them good training and a more pleasant work environment than other job opportunities that might have been open to them, such as fast food restaurants. Teens with higher personal career expectations saw their library work experience as a resume builder or as an asset on their college applications (Walter & Meyers, 2003).

A. Field Test in Library Youth Services

Dresang, Gross, and Holt (2006) used a national leadership grant from IMLS to develop and field test an outcome-based planning and evaluation (OBPE) model especially geared to library youth services. They field-tested their model at the Saint Louis Public Library and published the results in *Dynamic Youth Services through Outcome-Based Planning and Evaluation.* Their model, an adaptation of the logic model widely cited in guides to outcome evaluation, makes it clear that planning is an important and integral step in the process. These researchers show how outcomes flow logically from assessing community needs and the library's capacity for meeting those needs. In turn, the service response or program designed to meet those needs flows logically from the defined outcomes. The evaluation then provides data about whether the outcomes have been met and informs the next cycle of OBPE.

The team behind the OBPE model tested their methods on a specific program at the Saint Louis Public Library, and the results of this outcome-based evaluation are reported in the publication cited above. The program, Children's Access to and Use of Technology Evaluation (CATE), was an effort to learn how the digital divide affected low-income children in the city, to develop programs and services to bridge the divide for fourth through eighth grade students, and to develop the OBPE model for evaluating those services. Among the findings:

- Children were enthusiastic about using computers and thought they were more competent than they actually were.
- Children had little knowledge of the skills generally associated with information literacy.
- Children wanted more kid-friendly sites and activities.
- Boys and girls used computers differently but did not differ in their actual amount of usage.
- Computer users also valued other services and resources offered by the library.
- Teachers, parents, and children valued the library staff's assistance.

By clearly demonstrating the applicability of outcome-based planning and evaluation efforts to library services to children, Dresang *et al.* (2006) provided a useful foundation on which other evaluators and library professionals could build.

IV. Summer Reading Program Outcome Evaluations

Public libraries in the United States have been offering summer reading programs since the early 1900s (Locke, 1988). These reading promotion programs have been institutionalized as a basic service in many, if not most, public libraries. These programs were assumed to help children avoid the notorious "summer reading loss" that is well-documented in educational research. As Matthews (2010) pointed out, however, there was little research documenting the actual outcomes of summer reading programs. Libraries had been citing the one study conducted by Heyns (1978) that suggested that library summer reading programs helped to reduce summer learning loss. There was nothing more current until the Dominican study, *Public Library Summer Reading Programs Close the Reading Gap* (Roman, Carran, & Fiore, 2010) was published.

Funded by IMLS, the Dominican study was a product of partnerships between the Johns Hopkins University Center for Summer Learning, The Colorado State Library, and the Texas State Library and Archives Commission. It was piloted at three public libraries, with the full study conducted at 11 sites across the United States. An advisory committee provided oversight. The study targeted children entering fourth grade. Children were given pretests and posttests to determine their reading levels before and after their library's summer reading programs. While there were some limitations to the study, including participant attrition and the lack of a nonparticipant control group, the study nevertheless provided new data from a national sampling of summer reading programs.

Among the findings from the Dominican study was the unsurprising result that children who participated in library summer reading programs scored higher on reading achievement tests at the beginning of the following school year than did students who had not participated. Children who participated tended to include more girls, Caucasians, and representatives of higher socioeconomic levels than those who did not participate. They came from families with more books at home than those of nonparticipants, and they were more confident and enthusiastic readers than children who did not take part in summer reading programs (Roman *et al.*, 2010).

The Dominican study received a great deal of attention, being the first national study of summer reading that attempted to document the outcomes of this ubiquitous public library activity. There have, however, been other initiatives at the state level to capture the outcomes of library summer reading programs. The Colorado State Library, for example, offers mini-grants to public libraries that measure four related statewide outcomes, namely that children and teens will

- develop a habit of reading;
- think that reading is fun;
- become regular library users; and
- think that the Summer Reading Program has helped them read better.

In addition to quantifying results, Colorado librarians are asked to collect qualitative data about the four outcomes by talking to participants and their families. Although the results are reported to the Colorado State Library, they have not been disseminated to the profession (Colorado Summer Reading Program, n.d.).

V. The Case of the California Summer Reading Program

In California, the statewide Summer Reading Program is funded in part by an IMLS grant through the California State Library and is coordinated by the California Library Association. Participating libraries were asked to submit usage data but there was no effort to collect outcome data until 2008. At that time Natalie Cole, the program coordinator, convened an advisory group of librarians from throughout the state to consider the implementation of an outcome component.

A preliminary needs assessment had been done in a meeting of more than 80 librarians at the California Library Association Conference. The advisory group revisited those findings and agreed that the most common needs that public libraries were trying to meet with summer reading programs was the relative lack of reading for pleasure and low levels of library usage in the summer. The group developed desired outcomes based on those needs for three different age levels—preschool, school age, and teen. They designed methods for testing those outcomes using surveys, interviews, and focus groups. Those outcomes were tested at nine public library sites in 2009 and 2010.

The pilot test, conducted over two summers, helped to determine the next steps. Many of the participating libraries had suffered staff shortages because of the budget cuts that were prevalent all over California in 2009. The reduced levels of staffing had made it difficult to implement the data collection methods for all age levels. It became clear to the advisory group that compromises would have to be made between methodological rigor and practicality. The research design for 2011 would be what the consultant to the project has called "outcome evaluation light."

The advisory group decided to broaden the outcomes evaluation in 2011 to any California library that wished to participate. The preschool segment would be eliminated but families would be added into the mix. Libraries with summer reading programs that targeted children under five would report results as family participation. The result to be measured for school age, teen, adult, and family participants was limited to two outcomes. The first outcome was defined as: Children [teens/adults/families] belong to a community (broadly defined) of readers and library users. The advisory group liked the notion of creating a reading community at the library and felt that this outcome captured the essence of reading for pleasure that summer programs ideally encourage. *Outcome One* speaks to readers who are looking for a social setting in which they can interact with other readers. It also allowed for a more subtle interpretation of the library as a haven for those who find reading to be a more personal and private activity. It assumed that any child, teen, adult, or family group who chose to participate in a library summer reading program, identified with the library and with the summer program, thereby became part of a community of interest.

The concepts of community and libraries and reading are very closely linked. It is instructive to visit a library and watch how people of all ages interact with this public space. Parents read to their young children or spend time in the new Family Place sites popping up all over California and other parts of the United States. People help each other spontaneously at Internet stations. School children share homework assignments with classmates who forgot to bring the instructions home with them. Patrons chat with clerks as they check books in or out. Even people sitting quietly by themselves with a book or a magazine or their laptop in front of them seem to be enjoying the feeling of being part of a community.

Outcome One recognized that there are many kinds of communities besides the geographic ones in which we live. These communities of choice may be based on religion, voluntarism, hobbies, cultural or leisure activities, or ethnic pride. With new emphasis on community and community building in the Summer Reading Program, Californians are positioning the public library as a significant community of interest.

The librarians who had spearheaded the pilot project were still concerned about the many children and teens in their communities who were not being reached by their summer reading programs. Their experiences echoed findings from the Dominican study that children who participated in library summer reading programs were, for the most part, the library "regulars."

They were children who already liked to read and would probably read for pleasure during the summer whether there was a library program or not. Studies repeatedly showed that children from low-socioeconomic groups who were most likely to suffer from summer learning loss and were consistently underrepresented in summer reading programs. The Idaho Commission for Libraries had identified and tackled this problem with their "Bright Futures Summer Reading Opportunities: Reaching Underserved Children" (Idaho Commission for Libraries, 2011). California, however, had not articulated this need as an outcome for summer reading.

To solve this problem, the group adopted a second outcome, aimed at reaching out to the children, teens, and families who were not regular library users by articulating Outcome Two: [Desired number] of [underserved target group] participate in the summer reading program. Libraries would be encouraged to analyze their own communities and identify the underserved populations that they wanted to reach. For example, a library might frame their outreach outcome as: 20 children from the Recreation Center day camp participate in the summer reading program. Or, 30 Spanish-speaking children participate in the summer reading program.

With this stated outcome, the summer reading program in California became both an outcome- and outreach-based program. This second outcome was similar to simple output measures in that it asked librarians to set a quantitative target. The advisory group felt, however, that because it called for changes in behavior by a specific group of people it qualified as an outcome measure.

Outcome Two also built on the community orientation of Outcome One. It acknowledged that the library is an important node in a web of support services engaged in the increasingly difficult task of helping families raise healthy children. Through outreach, Summer Reading Programs can draw more people of all ages into that web so they can be nurtured by it and can be enabled to nurture others as well. Outcome Two was intended to institutionalize public library' ongoing efforts to open their hearts and minds and doors to every man, woman, and child in their service areas.

California libraries participating in the statewide program in 2010 were encouraged, but not required, to conduct the designated outcome evaluation. A webinar conducted in January, and available in its archived form since then, was attended by more than 120 people. It was designed to motivate people to take part, to give some basic information and training, and to direct people to the extensive web site devoted to the project (Introduction to California's Outcome-Based Summer Reading Program, 2010). This web site gives detailed background information, directions for collecting data through surveys, interviews, and focus groups, and tips for effective outreach efforts (California Summer Reading Program, 2011).

In spite of the best efforts of the coordinator and the advisory group, only 10 library jurisdictions (with a total of 224 branches) elected to participate in the outcomes evaluation aspect of the Summer Reading Program in 2011. However, between them, the participating libraries yielded an impressive amount of data.

School age children, the traditional audience for summer reading programs, were predictably the most heavily represented participants. Four thousand two hundred and ninety-nine children between the ages of 4 and 13 participated in the outcome evaluation. They were given a menu of descriptors for the library in the summer time:

- A place to see friends.
- A place to meet new friends.
- A place to find books to read.
- A place to find other things to read.
- A place for activities and shows.
- A place to do homework or study.
- A place to use computers.
- A community center.
- A friendly place.
- A fun place.
- An awesome place.
- A place for me.

They were allowed to check as many statements as they wanted. By far the largest number of responses—78%—went to "a place to find books to read." However, 42% said it was "a place to meet friends" and 60% said it was "a friendly place." These findings, taken with a 66% positive response to the statement that they "like to share books or talk about the books they read," were interpreted as indicators that Outcome One had been met. The summer reading program did seem to provide children with a feeling of belonging to a community of readers.

A smaller number of teens participated in the outcome effort—a total of 865 from 159 library branches. Even more teens than children described the library as a place to find books to read: 83%. More teens—65%—also found the library to be a place to find other things to read. This makes sense, given the number of teens who like to read magazines and online content. While only 43% of teens described the library as a place to see friends, nearly as many, 39%, said it was a place to meet new friends. And 68% of the teens said they liked to talk about the books they read.

Only 4 library jurisdictions, with a total of 63 branches, reported on family participation in summer reading. Two hundred sixty-six family surveys for *Outcome One* were returned. Ninety-four percent said the library is a place to find books to read. Fifty-two percent said the library is a place to see friends or other families, and 45% said that it is a place to meet new friends. This is consistent with the observations of many librarians that families with preschool children tend to develop relationships with the other families they meet at storytimes and other library activities. A whopping 92% said they like to share books or talk about the books they read.

The data for *Outcome Two* are a little harder to parse. Even fewer libraries chose to implement the outreach-oriented outcome. Six library jurisdictions reached a total of 1064 previously underserved children, teens, and families through special outreach efforts. The range of people served is impressive: 73 migrant children attending summer school in Imperial County, 15 teens at a Los Angeles residential drug rehabilitation program, 15 family members from a social service agency in a low-income community, 8 parents and children from a college day care program, 3 homeless adults and 23 ESL students in Long Beach, 40 recipients of the Sacramento Food Bank Summer Program, 90 parents and children in a Head Start program, 19 expectant and new parents in a low-income community in Santa Clara County.

While the numbers of libraries participating was a little disappointing, the positive comments from the librarians who took part helped to validate the value of the outcomes effort. One youth services coordinator welcomed the opportunity to develop a more intentional approach to summer reading in her system. Like several other managers, she also found that the data they received were welcomed by the library administrators, donors, and Board of Commissioners.

Many librarians reported significant lessons learned that will make a difference in how they implement aspects of the program next year, particularly the outreach component. Many reported that the experience led to new relationships with people working in various agencies that they partnered with during the summer. One librarian wrote,

> One very positive lesson: all our outreach for Summer Reading does have an accumulative effect. For example, two of the Head Starts that were visited this year were happy to hand over rosters to the librarian because last year a librarian had visited them, and they had a successful experience then so they were happy to do it again. Just shows the subtle effects that outreach does have in our favor.

Two different libraries found that teens responded to the volunteer opportunities that had been created for the Summer Reading Program and redesigned their teen programs accordingly.

In addition to the surveys reported briefly above, librarians were encouraged to hold focus groups with representative groups of summer reading participants. Those who did so were impressed with what they learned about what works and what doesn't work so well in their programming, promotion, and outreach. They became converts to this qualitative research method as a means to getting in-depth feedback from their patrons.

In general, many librarians have become convinced of the value of having good outcomes data, both to share with stakeholders and to use in making internal decisions about where to put resources. Some library administrators made good use of the information gathered to build support for the summer reading program. More than one respondent asked to see the statewide data so they could see how their own library compared.

The coordinator of California's Summer Reading Program, Natalie Cole, hopes to at least double the number of libraries participating during 2012. It would be helpful to be able to offer some kind of incentive for participation, but funding for that is not available. However, word is beginning to spread about the benefits of participating in both the outcome and outreach components. Last year's participants are proving to be excellent recruiters. They can speak first-hand about how relatively easy it was to implement and how useful the results have been.

VI. Conclusion

The challenge of making outcome evaluation a standard aspect of youth services is that it is still perceived as a complex—and optional—activity by many practitioners. When evaluation is required by a funding agency, most will look for an outside professional to do the work. What Dresang *et al.* (2006) did with their OBPE model and what the organizers of the outcome- and outreach-based California Summer Reading Program tried to do, was to make this tool available to front-line librarians and youth services coordinators. California librarians who conducted outcome evaluations of their summer reading programs learned that this is not rocket science and that it yields enormously useful information about their work. It contributed to a more intentional and focused approach to a program that had been conducted without much thought for decades.

Having worked now for three years to implement a soft launch of an outcome- and outreach-based Summer Reading Program, California's proponents now recognize that ongoing education is needed in order to convince more librarians to embrace this approach. Without monetary incentives to offer, state organizers must communicate the benefits to organizations that adopt outcome evaluation as a standard management tool. In every print- and web-based promotional piece and at every training opportunity, they repeat the benefits which accrue. They repeat that outcome-based summer reading programs:

- Demonstrate meaningful results.
- Are relevant to the local community.
- Attract funding.
- Build capacity among staff.
- Contribute to improved management decision making.

In addition California Summer Reading Program organizers are being even more proactive about training librarians in the skills needed to implement it. California libraries have been particularly hard hit by budget cuts, and many librarians are doing the work previously done by two or three professionals. Some have said that they just cannot contemplate doing anything different or new. Therefore it is hard to convince them that proving the positive impacts of their services on their customers can help to compete for funding in bad economic times.

As noted earlier, in California, methods for data collection have been streamlined to one short survey to be completed at the end of the summer by at least 100 participants along with 2 focus groups for each age level targeted by the program. Tips for doing these have been posted on the web site and repeated in training workshops and webinars. Perhaps the most effective tool for convincing people that they can do this, however, has been the testimony of librarians who have done it. Their voices speak eloquently about the relative ease and value of outcome evaluation as a means to capture the results of the good work that youth services librarians do.

References

California Summer Reading Program. (2011). Retrieved from http://www.cla-net. org/displaycommon.cfm?an=1&subarticlenbr=64

Colorado Summer Reading Program: Outcome-Based Evaluation (OBE) Information. (n.d.). Retrieved from http://www.cde.state.co.us/cdelib/summerreading/Downloads/pdf/OBE_information.pdf

Dresang, E. T., Gross, M., & Holt, L. E. (2006). *Dynamic youth services through outcome-based planning and evaluation*. Chicago, IL: American Library Association.

Heyns, B. (1978). *Summer learning and the effects of schooling*. New York, NY: Academic Press.

Himmel, E. E., & Wilson, W. J. (1998). *Planning for results: A public library transformation process*. Chicago, IL: American Library Association.

Idaho Commission for Libraries. (2011). *Bright futures reading opportuntities: Reaching underserved children*. Boise, ID: Author.

Introduction to California's outcome-based summer reading program [webinar]. (2010). Retrieved from http://infopeople.org/training/introduction_California's-outcome/based-summer-reading-program

Locke, J. L. (1988). *The effectiveness of summer reading programs in public libraries in the United States.* Doctoral dissertation. University of Pittsburgh, Pittsburgh, PA.

Matthews, J. (2010). Evaluating summer reading programs: Suggested improvements. *Public Libraries, 49*(4), 34–40.

McClure, C. R., Owen, A., Zweizig, D. L., Lynch, M. J., & Van House, N. A. (1987). *Planning and role setting for public libraries: A manual of options and procedures.* Chicago, IL: American Library Association.

Meyers, E. (2002). Youth development and libraries: A conversation with Karen Pittman. *Public Libraries, 41*(September–October), 256–260.

Nelson, S. (2001). *New planning for results: A streamlined approach.* Chicago, IL: American Library Association.

Nelson, S. (2008). *Strategic planning for results.* Chicago, IL: American Library Association.

Roman, S., Carran, D. T., & Fiore, C. D. (2010). *The Dominican study: Public library summer reading programs close the reading gap.* River Forest, IL: Dominican University Graduate School of Library and Information Science. Retrieved from http://www.dom.edu/academics/gslis/downloads/DOM_IMLS_BOOK_2010_FINAL_web.pdf

Sweeney, J. K. (2010, November). State of library evaluation in California 2010. Paper presented at the California Library Association Conference, Sacramento, CA.

Van House, N. A., Lynch, M. J., McClure, C. R., Zweizig, D. L., & Rodger, E. J. (1987). *Output measures for public libraries: A manual of standardized procedures* (2nd ed.). Chicago, IL: American Library Association.

Walter, V. A. (1992). *Output measures for public library service to children: A manual of standardized procedures.* Chicago, IL: American Library Association.

Walter, V. A. (1995). *Output measures and more: Planning and evaluating public library services for young adults.* Chicago, IL: American Library Association.

Walter, V. A., & Meyers, E. (2003). *Teens and libraries: Getting it right.* Chicago, IL: American Library Association.

Needs Analyses and Results

Assessment in a Medium-Sized Academic Library: A Success Story

Carolyn Gutierrez and Jianrong Wang
Library, The Richard Stockton College of New Jersey, Galloway, NJ, USA

Abstract

This case study demonstrates the positive changes that evolved from a series of assessment activities. It shows that even smaller libraries can conduct assessment, with the support of colleagues and the library administration. Librarians can take a proactive role rather than waiting for a mandate from college administration. Two years of LibQUAL+® survey results (2005 and 2008) were analyzed in depth using statistical correlation analyses. Following this, respondents' comments were categorized by dimension and analyzed to detect correlations. The information collected was then used to track trends and highlight the strengths and weaknesses of the library through the eyes of its users. A comparison of the survey results showed an increase in perceived service in all dimensions. However, user expectations rose even faster, especially with regard to e-resources, equipment, and study space. Positive results about staff expertise and service attitudes demonstrated that users valued the personal attention and capabilities of the library staff. The study shows that a user survey is only the first step in an assessment process. Assessment can be effective only if follow-up actions are taken to address negative feedback and the actions then communicated to all stakeholders. While assessment has become a necessity for many libraries, small- and medium-sized libraries often shy away from it, due to limited resources. The Richard Stockton College Library undertook assessment in areas in which it could expect achievable results. Another outcome came in the form of additional resources, which narrowed the gap between library services and users needs.

Keywords: Academic libraries; library assessment; evaluation; LibQUAL+®; data analysis

I. Introduction

In this period of tightened budgets and relatively free access to information online, academic librarians are discovering that the central role of the library in their institutions is no longer a given. It is necessary now to justify its position with tangible evidence of the library's contributions to the mission of their institutions.

CONTEXTS FOR ASSESSMENT AND OUTCOME EVALUATION IN LIBRARIANSHIP
ADVANCES IN LIBRARIANSHIP, VOL. 35
© 2012 by Emerald Group Publishing Limited
ISSN: 0065-2830
DOI: 10.1108/S0065-2830(2012)0000035007

The Richard Stockton College of New Jersey (RSC) is a liberal arts college with over 8000 students located in southern New Jersey. The library staff consists of 3 administrators, 5 librarians, 18 full-time staff and 10 part-time. Although the library participated in LibQUAL+® surveys and assessment of certain individual services, such as pre- and post-testing of student learning in information literacy sessions and analysis of periodical usage, an in-depth assessment of library services as a whole had never been undertaken.

In the summer of 2008 a Faculty Resource Network (FRN) seminar on library assessment at New York University, attended by the authors, transformed attitudes about assessment by a library. Conference conveners, Hiller and Self (2008), emphasized using assessment creatively and adopting a positive, rather than defensive attitude toward findings, even if they are negative. They introduced seminar participants to the merits and applications of assessment, and stressed that lack of a statistical background was not a barrier. Everyone and every department in a library can conduct and benefit from assessment on some level. Assessment can provide the opportunity to tell the library's story to administrators, emphasizing not only its strengths but its weaknesses. It becomes part of an ongoing process toward improving library services and meeting user needs. According to the seminar conveners, whatever type of assessment libraries employ, following up on the results is crucial to success. Stakeholders need to be informed of the results and of measures taken to remediate the problems identified through assessment.

Neither of the Stockton librarians attending the FRN seminar had a statistical background. Nevertheless, they returned to work with enthusiasm about assessment. They initiated a meeting of library faculty and administrators and persuaded them about its value and, as a result, a Library Assessment Committee was established consisting of the library director, two associate directors, five librarians, and the coordinator of information technology.

Although there are diverse ways to carry out assessment, many libraries use LibQUAL+®, a web-based assessment tool that collects and interprets library users' perceptions of library service quality. Since the RSC library administered LibQUAL+® in 2005 and 2008, the Assessment Committee decided to start with an analysis of that data.

In both surveys, users expressed satisfaction with the services provided by the library staff but had some negative views about Information Control and Library as a Place. In 2005 the library administration reviewed the LibQUAL+® results and shared them with the professional staff. Some changes were made, notably in the establishment of a Graduate Student Lounge and increased library hours, but there the analysis more or less ended. The 2008 results showed some improvement, but the expectations of users had increased even more. The changes made as a result of the 2005 responses did not seem to be adequately reflected in the 2008 survey, which was disappointing. "We responded and gave them what they wanted and they're still unhappy" was the general sentiment expressed. The LibQUAL+® survey was again relegated to the shelf. This time the Assessment Committee took a different approach.

A. Literature Review

Since the focus of this article is not just assessment but also about *using* the results, the authors examined how other libraries utilized their LibQUAL+® findings. LibQUAL+® provides a quantitative representation of respondents perceptions of library services but does not address the questions *"Why* do they feel that way?" or *"How* should we improve our services?" It is what libraries do with the LibQUAL+® analysis that can lead to evidence-based change. A detailed analysis of respondent comments or a follow-up with qualitative research can fill these gaps.

Gerke and Maness (2010) in their LibQUAL+® analysis discovered which factors correlated with a high rate of satisfaction with the electronic resources collection namely, patron age, discipline, frequency of library web site use, and frequency of visits to the physical library. Interestingly, they found it was not a person's age or discipline that made a significant difference, but frequency of their use of the library web site. The more attractive libraries with study space available also had the highest rate of on-site use. They found a link between the frequency of library visits and satisfaction with electronic resources. This suggests that use of a library's physical space and its web site are not divorced from their level of satisfaction with the electronic resources collection. They may in fact reinforce one another. Gerke and Maness' study refutes the argument that brick and mortar libraries will soon become obsolete.

LibQUAL+® results can also be helpful when analyzed prior to a strategic planning process. Saunders (2008) discusses the value of drilling down into the LibQUAL+® data in preparation for strategic planning. LibQUAL+® data offer a contemporary snapshot of how patrons view their library, while strategic planning focuses on where the library should be in 5 or 10 years. Prior to their LibQUAL+® survey, Purdue librarians had an anecdotal understanding of patron use and perceptions, but the LibQUAL+® data helped them to produce a balanced strategic plan based on fact, not merely impression.

Another way of approaching the LibQUAL+® data is to examine the differences in patrons and their expectations. Jones and Kayongo (2008) reported that Notre Dame's libraries found users' comments extremely helpful in shedding light on the quantitative data. They discovered, after examining and mapping them to the LibQUAL+® survey questions, that under-graduates, graduates, and faculty had differing needs and expectations. For undergraduates, access to the physical library, despite the availability of remote access to electronic resources, was still important. They wanted the library to be open 24 hours for studying and appreciated the personal attention received from library staff. Graduate students, on the other hand, were more concerned with print and/or electronic journal collection coverage and much less concerned with services or the physical library. Faculty echoed the graduate student concerns, but expressed their dissatisfaction with the size of the collections even more vehemently. Both groups voiced unhappiness with the recall policy when books were checked out of the library. In response, Notre Dame revised their recall policy, introduced 24-hour access during study weeks, and renovated the Graduate Student area.

Heath, Kyrillidou, and Askew (2004) provide an excellent compilation of articles on how libraries utilized their LibQUAL+® findings. One of the entries (Knapp, 2004) emphasized the importance of adopting a positive approach to the findings. Instead of reacting defensively to negative res-ponses, Knapp's library system drew on the results to redesign public services at the University of Pittsburgh Library System. To increase student satis-faction with the quality of service, they launched new initiatives such as digital reference service, a targeted instruction program, and a Peer-to-Peer Library Consultants Program.

Of particular interest was the way in which Lewis (2009) at East Carolina University, tied in their LibQUAL+® results with student inform-ation literacy outcomes. Local questions added to the survey were specifically designed to garner information on how their information literacy program contributed to student learning and academic success.

Those surprised and dismayed with lower scores after switching to LibQUAL+® Lite from LibQUAL+® are directed to an evaluation of how sampling in LibQUAL+® Lite can affect scoring (Thompson, Kyrillidou, & Cook, 2009). The authors provide linking equations to convert scores from the traditional LibQUAL+® items into the LibQUAL+® Lite protocol.

II. Data Analysis at Stockton

Both quantitative and qualitative analyses were utilized in analyzing the two years of results at Stockton. Quantitative data from LibQUAL+® elicited information on how users felt about the library services, while the qualitative data from comments indicated why users rated the services as they did, and where and how they would like the services to be improved.

A. Quantitative Analysis

The LibQUAL+® survey deals with three dimensions which are *Affect of Service, Information Control,* and *Library as Place* which are detailed in Appendix A. Statistical correlation analysis was used to compare 2005 and 2008 results to determine if there were any trends. Dimensions were analyzed by user groups and each question was correlated with its ratings of the five means (minimum, desired, perceived, adequacy, and superiority) defined by LibQUAL+®. Significance was sought through comparing rating changes reflected in each dimensional questions made by user categories. To benchmark Stockton library service ratings, results were also compared with academic libraries in the Virtual Academic Library Environment (VALE), a NJ state consortium. The goal was threefold: (1) to identify areas in which feasible improvements might be made; (2) to offer constructive suggestions on how those improvements might be accomplished; and (3) to highlight areas that met with user approval. The results were as follows:

1. *Improved user services*
    Faculty, students, and staff perceived that library service overall had improved in 2008. All three dimensions were rated higher in 2008 than in 2005. This was particularly true of Affect of Service in which all questions were rated significantly higher (Fig. 1).

2. *Rising expectations*
    Correlated with the rising score of perceived services were the rising expectations. Data from the 2005 and 2008 surveys indicated that, overall, users' minimum and desired expectations were rising, and rising faster than perceived services. Expectations in areas of Affect of Service, such as remote access to e-resources, making information easily accessible for independent use, library as a getaway for study, learning or research were significantly higher (Fig. 2).

3. *Greater demand for resources*
    The Adequacy gap score showed that the library was struggling to meet the minimum expectations of users in Information Control and Library as Place. "Print and/or electronic

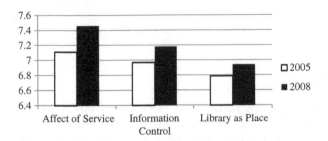

Fig. 1 Perceived services, 2005 and 2008.
Source: LibQUAL+® Survey: Richard Stockton College of New Jersey, 2005 and 2008.

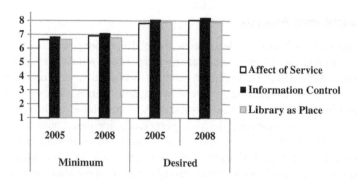

Fig. 2   Expectations of services, minimum vs. desired, 2005 and 2008.
Source: LibQUAL+® Survey: Richard Stockton College of New Jersey, 2005 and 2008.

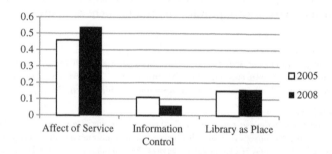

Fig. 3   Adequacy gap (perceived services—minimum expectations), 2005 and 2008.
Source: LibQUAL+® Survey: Richard Stockton College of New Jersey, 2005 and 2008.

journal collections I require for my work" was rated lower in 2008 than 2005, suggesting a greater gap between the user expectation for services and the services that users perceived they were receiving. It was also evident that resource accessibility was regarded as important. The gap was also greater in describing the library as "a getaway for study, learning or research" and "community space for group learning and group study" (Fig. 3).

B. Benchmarking

Eleven VALE libraries participated in the 2008 LibQUAL+® survey (see Appendix B), including Stockton. Among them were seven colleges and universities and four community colleges. The total number of respondents was 4475. Because there was no separate VALE data available excluding RSC data, the data provided in this article are a relative comparison.

Compared with other VALE institutions, RSC ranked higher in Perceived Service Means, Affect of Service, especially in "Employees who instill confidence in users" (0.37 higher) and "Employees who are consistently courteous" (0.34 higher) as shown in Fig. 4. However, RSC was rated lower in Information Control and Library as Place as indicated in Figs. 5 and 6.

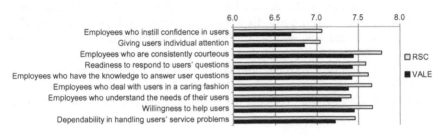

Fig. 4 Perceived service means, affect of service, RSC vs. VALE.
Source: LibQUAL+® Survey: VALE and Richard Stockton College of New Jersey, 2008.

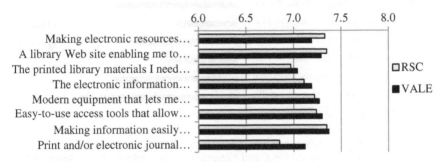

Fig. 5 Perceived service means, information control, RSC vs. VALE.
Source: LibQUAL+® Survey: VALE and Richard Stockton College of New Jersey, 2008.

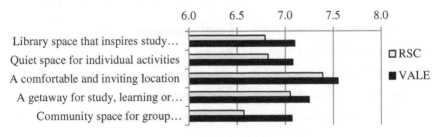

Fig. 6 Perceived service means, library as place, RSC vs. VALE.
Source: LibQUAL+® Survey: VALE and Richard Stockton College of New Jersey, 2008.

Except for "Making electronic resources accessible from my home or office" and "A library web site enabling me to locate information on my own" in Information Control that were positive ratings, the rest of the ratings in these two dimensions all received negative scores. Library as Place was rated much lower, especially in "Library space that inspires study and learning" which was 0.31 point lower, and "Community space for group learning and group study" dropped half of a point. The Adequacy gap scores (Perceived Mean—Minimum Expectation), shown in Figs. 7 and 8, also demonstrated that RSC was behind VALE in these two dimensions. Among the areas, "Modern equipment that lets me easily access needed information" and "Print and/or electronic journal collections I require for my work" RSC received negative scores, −0.05 and −0.32 respectively. This is not surprising because the college has been expanding, both in academic

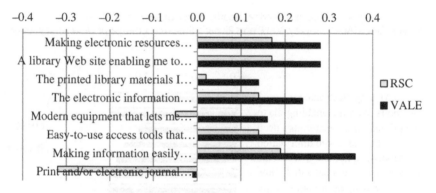

Fig. 7 Adequacy gap, information control, RSC vs. VALE.
Source: LibQUAL+® Survey: VALE and Richard Stockton College of New Jersey, 2008.

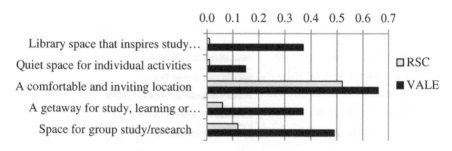

Fig. 8 Adequacy gap, library as place, RSC vs. VALE.
Source: LibQUAL+® Survey: VALE and Richard Stockton College of New Jersey, 2008.

programs and size of student body, while the library has remained unchanged in terms of facilities and budget.

C. Qualitative Analysis

In August and September 2008, the Library Assessment Committee analyzed comments made by respondents in the 2008 LibQUAL+® survey. The 2008 report was chosen because we wanted to know what the differences were following the 2005 survey. Of the 411 total respondents, 182 offered comments that related to all service areas. As indicated in Table 1 undergraduates made the most comments. The Committee categorized the comments by the LibQUAL+® dimensions, and the librarian members

Table 1
Respondents Who Offered Comments by User Group, 2008

User group	No. of respondents
Undergraduate	110
Faculty	32
Graduate	23
Staff	15
Library staff	2
Total	*182*

Source: LibQUAL+® Survey: Richard Stockton College of New Jersey, 2008.

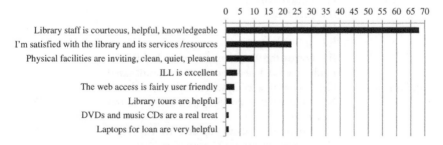

Fig. 9 Number of positive comments (112).
Source: LibQUAL+® Survey: Richard Stockton College of New Jersey, 2008.

Table 2
Comments by Dimensions, 2008

Dimensions	Comments	Year 2008
Affect of Service	Library staff is courteous, helpful, knowledgeable	68
	I'm satisfied with the library/services	23
	Library staff is not helpful	4
	Library staff is not courteous or don't want to be bothered	3
	Library staff is loud	3
	Library needs more staff	2
	Students need help from reference librarians	2
Information Control		
Resources	DVDs and music CDs are a real treat	1
	Need more journals, (full-text) e-journals, online databases, e-books	1
	Inadequate collection; lack of research/program/language materials	22
	Outdated books and movie collection	13
	Needs popular fiction, genealogy, and other books like public libraries	11
	Need multiple copies of daily newspapers same day mornings	2
	Need to increase budget	2
	Need more DVDs	2
Access	Databases are not user-friendly or easily accessible	3
	Web site has been VASTLY improved in recent years	7
	ILS is hard to use; needs instruction to use	5
	Need more users allowed for database	4
	Library tours are helpful	3
	Need to inform faculty of new materials/equipment	2
	Hate microfiche!!!	2
	ILL excellent	1
	ILL wait is too long	4
	ILL unfilled	3
	ILL borrowing limits make research difficult	2
	Finding what I need becomes so complicated	1
Equipment	Need more/new computers, laptops, and outlets	1
	Need more faster/working printers, more free printing	17
	Need more/new photo copiers; free copying	15
	Need more software on computers	5

Table 2. (*Continued*)

Dimensions	Comments	Year 2008
	Need to save paper (double-sided printing)	1
	The stapler could be replaced	1
Library as Place	Physical facilities are inviting, quiet, pleasant	10
	Inadequate space, need more group study rooms	10
	Study rooms need whiteboards	20
	Need longer hours; nights and weekends	16
	Physical layout/facilities unwelcoming	15
	Poor lighting	6
	Uncomfortable furniture/furniture layout	4
	Shortage of seating	3
	Poor layout/signage in stacks	2
	Need library map handy or better signage	1
	Improve display cases/displays	1
	Open snack bar would be great	1
	Exit on upper level that provides a convenient [sic] exit should be allowed to use	1
	Total	326

Source: LibQUAL+® Survey: Richard Stockton College of New Jersey, 2008.

volunteered to adopt areas to be analyzed. When the librarians reported their findings to the Committee, they were also required to bring suggestions on how to solve the problems they identified. The Committee was delighted to learn that there were many positive comments from students, faculty, and staff complimenting library staff on their job performance (Fig. 9). Echoing the quantitative results, Affect of Service was rated highest among the three dimensions.

There were a minority of comments indicating that staff members were loud, and that certain students did not get the help that they expected. The majority of complaints about Information Control focused on outdated collections and inadequate resources and equipment. Complaints about Library as Place included lack of space and, particularly lack of group study rooms, insufficient seating, and poor lighting. Noise was also singled out as a major problem. Table 2 details the comments in respective areas. Of the total 326 comments on the library services that divided into the three dimensions, the list under Information Control was the longest (Figs. 10 and 11).

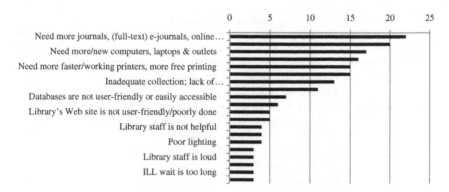

Fig. 10 Negative comments (201).
Source: LibQUAL+® Survey: Richard Stockton College of New Jersey, 2008.

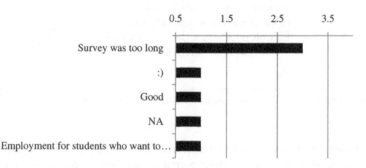

Fig. 11 Neutral comments (7).
Source: LibQUAL+® Survey: Richard Stockton College of New Jersey, 2008.

D. Resulting Actions

The library had asked for feedback, and it received it. Now what should be done? The Committee decided to tackle first those areas that seemed to be easily achievable, or less budget-constrained, such as Library as Place. After examining the problem areas that were revealed in the survey results, the Committee recommended a list of actions with timelines to track progress. The librarians volunteered to take on the tasks and through collective effort, the library completed the following actions:

1. *Arranged for focus group sessions to follow-up on the LibQUAL+® results*
   The survey results showed that graduate students was the group most unhappy with Library as Place. The Information Literacy librarian worked with the Director of the Institute for College

Teaching, who is also a faculty member in the Psychology program, to plan two focus group sessions with graduate students. A list of questions designed to find out the reason for graduate students dissatisfaction was developed. The Director of the Institute, who had experience running focus groups, moderated the two sessions. Although the questions were used as a starting point, the students were also encouraged to comment freely. The sessions were audio taped and later transcribed by two librarians. Results revealed that graduate students desired a larger lounge and more resources relevant to their fields, particularly journals. Since the majority of graduate students held full-time jobs, they would also prefer the library to be open longer hours, even on weekends. These findings concurred with what Jones and Kayongo (2008) found in their study.

2. *Focused on accessibility*
Data suggested that access to electronic resources was the weakest link in the library's services. To strengthen this area, an electronic coordinator position was created to be responsible for all aspects related to electronic databases. The library also streamlined the staff's responsibilities to enable more emphasis to the library's web site and digital initiations.

3. *Created video tutorials on using library resources and Chat Reference*
Both faculty and students expressed a need to know how to use the library resources. Online Camtasia video tutorials, accessible to students through the Library home page, were created to guide users in searching electronic databases. Students can view them at their convenience and from anywhere with Internet access so that they can learn at their own pace. In addition, "Chat with a Librarian" was activated on the library web site from 6 to 10 p.m. on weekdays to create virtual reference service.

4. *Surveyed interlibrary loan users and planned ways of accelerating service*
Although interlibrary loan service received positive ratings in the surveys, there were still complaints regarding the length of waiting time. Since the library had borrowers access information, it was easy to contact them via e-mail and solicit feedback. Only 26 responded, but those who did generally expected articles to arrive much more quickly. To address this complaint, the library implemented Ariel software to speed up the process. Students have voiced their approval of the speed with which requests for periodical articles are filled now, sometimes arriving in their e-mail as an attachment within a day or two.

5. *Initiated lighting improvements*
The library had a history of poor lighting since its renovation in 1995. Due to the lighting design, the library was dark and gloomy in some areas. This not only negatively affected the attractiveness of the library, but hampered book browsing and retrieval in the stacks. The Assessment Committee put this problem on the top of its action list. It was reported to the Provost who asked members of his staff to walk through the library and report back on lighting and space issues. The Associate Vice Provost noted the poor lighting in the library stacks and that the lamps were outdated. He recommended replacing the old lighting fixtures. The Provost provided special funds and over the next six months, plant management replaced all the bulbs with better, more energy-efficient bulbs that brightened the shadowy corners of the library.

6. *Identified underutilized space and reconfigured space usage*
With the advancement of technology and changes in user trends, certain parts of the library were underutilized, like the fixed rows of carrels without electric outlets. Yet they occupied prime space in the reference area on the main level. Each of the librarians undertook to examine the library's use of space and report back to the Assessment Committee with their findings as well as suggestions for improvement. The little-used carrels, blocking the light and

view from the windows, were replaced with round tables. This change transformed the reference room into a brighter, more open, and inviting area. Changes were also made in other areas such as the former business reference section, where print business indexes were replaced by video viewing stations. The College Administration was made aware of the library's needs and incorporated it in their budget and space planning. One important victory, the College Administration returned several group study rooms, which had been used as faculty offices, to the library.

7. *Beautification of the Library*
   Art Department faculty members offered advice and donated student artwork to beautify the library. The Provost's office designated special funding for new carpeting on the main level of the library. The new carpet not only brightens the library lobby and hallway, but also tones down the noise level, sending out a cheering message to users.

Other aspects of the library were addressed as well. A meeting of the entire library staff was held to inform them of the LibQUAL+® results. Staff members were asked to be mindful when talking in public areas as well as in offices in order to control the noise level. Librarians targeted other areas and incorporated them as assessment projects. These included a study of overlap in print and electronic journal subscriptions, an online catalog usability test, a study of distance education student learning modules, and an assessment of student research methods. These projects resulted in spending the material budget more efficiently, a greater understanding of student perceptions and usage of the online catalog, and knowing the needs of the students during their learning processes.

In 2011 the library undertook a LibQUAL+® survey again. Results showed an increase in graduate students satisfaction, indicating that the follow-up actions were bearing fruit. Users were less unhappy about the space, but still hoped for a quieter library. As of preparation of this chapter, other possibilities were being investigated such as designating more spaces for quiet study.

Further, the library folded assessment into the library's five-year review process and report. This task was easier than expected due to the completed assessment work and documented accomplishments. The library's mission and goals were reexamined during the review process, and vision, value, and future plans were established. An overall assessment plan, which included all departments and service points, was being developed at the end of 2011 and a true user-centered library was under discussion.

III. Conclusion

The above accomplishments could not have been achieved without college-wide support which was realized through the assessment process. At college-wide meetings, librarians reported on survey results and voiced the concerns that users had expressed. Most importantly, they presented their findings to the Deans Council and the President, informing them about student and faculty issues. Such communication was effective because it focused on what students and faculty needed, rather than what librarians said was needed. As a result, support from the administration was achieved. In addition library resources became a required element in proposals for new academic programs.

Following through on user feedback was also a vital step in Stockton's library assessment, a step that was also very difficult. However, with enthusiastic librarians and supportive administrators, this mission was accomplished. Librarians served in many roles in these processes including those of gentle prodders, patron advocates, investigators, creative problem solvers, catalysts for change, assessment learners, and educators.

Although this was a local study, the overall results have general applicability. LibQUAL+® provided a springboard to initiate assessment, even though Stockton did not have an assessment specialist on staff, nor librarians with a statistical background. It afforded librarians an opportunity for professional growth and direct involvement in the assessment process. The process also resulted in additional resources being given to the library based on direct user expressions of need, a highly significant outcome of the needs assessment process.

Acknowledgments

The authors would like to thank members of the Richard Stockton College of NJ Library Assessment Committee for their support and hard work in the assessment activities.

Appendix A: LibQUAL+® Dimensions

Affect of Service (AS)

[AS-1] Employees who instill confidence in users
[AS-2] Giving users individual attention
[AS-3] Employees who are consistently courteous
[AS-4] Readiness to respond to users' questions
[AS-5] Employees who have the knowledge to answer user questions
[AS-6] Employees who deal with users in a caring fashion
[AS-7] Employees who understand the needs of their users
[AS-8] Willingness to help users
[AS-9] Dependability in handling users' service problems

Information Control (IC)

[IC-1] Making electronic resources accessible from my home or office
[IC-2] A library web site enabling me to locate information on my own
[IC-3] The printed library materials I need for my work
[IC-4] The electronic information resources I need
[IC-5] Modern equipment that lets me easily access needed information
[IC-6] Easy-to-use access tools that allow me to find things on my own
[IC-7] Making information easily accessible for independent use
[IC-8] Print and/or electronic journal collections I require for my work

Library as Place (LP)

[LP-1] Library space that inspires study and learning
[LP-2] Quiet space for individual activities
[LP-3] A comfortable and inviting location
[LP-4] A getaway for study, learning or research
[LP-5] Community space for group learning and group study

Appendix B: VALE Libraries Participating in the 2008 LibQUAL+® Survey

Institution	Respondents (*n*)
College or University	
1. FDU	389
2. Monmouth Univ.	324
3. NJM Sprague Library	430
4. Richard Stockton College of New Jersey	411
5. Rowan University	113
6. The College of New Jersey	1035
7. William Paterson University	383
Sub total	*3085*
Community College	
8. Bergen Community College	683
9. Cumberland	245
10. RVCC	156
11. UCC	306
Sub total	*1390*
Grand total	*4475*

References

Gerke, J., & Maness, J. M. (2010). The physical and the virtual: The relationship between library as place and electronic collections. *College & Research Libraries*, *71*(1), 20–31.

Heath, F., Kyrillidou, M., & Askew, C. A. (Eds.). (2004). *Libraries act on their LibQUAL+™ findings: From data to action*. Binghamton, NY: Haworth Information Press.

Hiller, S., & Self, J. (2008, June 9–13). Library assessment: Measuring and documenting the library's contributions to academic success. Seminar presented at the Faculty Resource Network, New York University, New York, NY. Retrieved from http://www.nyu.edu/frn/programs.events/enrichment/network.summer.2008.html#seminar-8

Jones, S., & Kayongo, J. (2008). Identifying student and faculty needs through LibQual+™: An analysis of qualitative survey comments. *College & Research Libraries*, *69*(6), 493–509.

Knapp, A. E. (2004). We asked them what they thought, now what do we do? The use of LibQUAL+™ data to redesign public services at the University of Pittsburgh. In F. Heath, M. Kyrillidou & C. A. Askew (Eds.), *Libraries act on their LibQUAL+™ findings: From data to action* (pp. 157–171). Binghamton, NY: Haworth Information Press.

Lewis, J. (2009, August 31). LibQUAL Spring 2009. Paper presented at East Carolina University, Greenville, NC. Retrieved from http://thescholarship.ecu.edu/bitstream/handle/10342/2177/LibQual%2b%202009%20PPT.pdf?sequence=1

LibQUAL+® Survey. (2005). Richard Stockton College of New Jersey.

LibQUAL+® Survey. (2008). Richard Stockton College of New Jersey.

LibQUAL+® Survey. (2008). VALE.

Saunders, E. S. (2008). Drilling the LibQUAL+® data for strategic planning [Special issue]. *Performance Measurement and Metrics*, *9*(3), 160–170. doi:10.1108/14678040810928390

Thompson, B., Kyrillidou, M., & Cook, C. (2009). Item sampling in service quality assessment surveys to improve response rates and reduce respondent burden: The "LibQUAL+® Lite" example. *Performance Measurement and Metrics*, *10*(1), 6–16. doi:10.1108/14678040910949657

Using Needs Assessment to Develop Research and Grant Support Services

Ricardo R. Andrade and Christine E. Kollen

Libraries, University of Arizona, Tucson, AZ, USA

Abstract

As any library strives to improve services and make them increasingly relevant, planning for change has become routine. During 2011, the University of Arizona's Libraries undertook extensive assessments in order to develop and improve services in support of research and grant services so that campus-wide achievements in research, scholarship, and creative works could improve. A project explored ways for the library to become more effective at increasing research and grant support to faculty, researchers, and graduate students in a scalable way, and to help the campus increase achievements in research, scholarship, and creative works. The project defined the library's role in research and grant activities and explored ways for the library to be involved at optimal points in these cycles. This chapter discusses the process developed for assessing what new research and grant support services the library might want to develop. This involved interviewing peer university libraries and surveying faculty and graduate students at the University of Arizona about their research and grant needs. The chapter also describes how results were analyzed to identify potential new library services. The project team recommended new services which were presented to the library for inclusion in its Strategic Plan. The methodology presented in this chapter can be used by any type of library for developing new services to include in their strategic plans.

Keywords: Academic libraries; needs assessment; strategic planning; research support services; grant support services

I. Introduction

The University of Arizona has two campuses, the main campus in Tucson and the south campus in Sierra Vista with a total of 39,901 students and 2855 faculty members in fiscal year 2010/2011. The University of Arizona Libraries (UAL) consists of the Main Library, the Center for Creative Photography, and the Science-Engineering and Fine Arts libraries. There are

© 2012 by Emerald Group Publishing Limited
ISSN: 0065-2830
DOI: 10.1108/S0065-2830(2012)0000035008

83

42 library faculty, 14 year-to-year academic professionals, and 95 classified staff members. In 2007, UAL appointed a Restructuring Project Team (RPT) to review the current and future work of the libraries to determine how UAL could be organized to accomplish changed or new work. As the charge to the team stated, "... our customers are doing more work in the electronic environment, the focus of our work is moving away from traditional collection development in most disciplines and small-scale, in-person instruction toward development and management of electronic information and development and use of scalable education tools" (University of Arizona Libraries, 2007, pp. 1–2). One of the deliverables for the project team was to develop "an organizational design that will enable the Libraries to accomplish strategic work with maximum efficiency and effectiveness with the staff available after budget cuts have been determined" (p. 4). One of the early decisions made by the RPT included reducing the number of UAL teams from 11 to 8. This was partly accomplished by consolidating three teams (Science-Engineering Team (SET), Social Sciences Team (SST), and Fine Arts/Humanities Team (FA/H)) into one new team: Research Support Services Team (RSST). RSST was assigned the following work:

- Subject liaisons/connection development;
- Content management/subject specialty;
- Education and instruction;
- Information resource management;
- Subject-specific research and reference assistance;
- Identifying needs and explore options for grant funding; and
- Participating in the library's strategic planning process (University of Arizona Libraries, Restructuring Team, 2008, p. 1).

Librarians from the three previous teams (SET, SST, and FA/H) were assigned to RSST, which had fewer librarians than the three previous teams. Some of the librarians originally assigned to SET, SST, and FA/H were assigned to teams other than RSST, such as the Instructional Services Team and the Administration Team. The new UAL organizational structure is detailed in Fig. 1. Even though the RPT defined the new structure of teams and what each team's responsibilities were, it was up to each team to determine how to accomplish its work. As is typical in many college and university libraries, librarians in subject-based teams had provided service to the campus through a liaison model, that is, each librarian provided instruction, reference, collection development, and connection development in their assigned departments or units. RSST made a decision to organize the team's responsibilities around function rather than this traditional liaison model.

University Libraries and Center for Creative Photography
University of Arizona
Organization Chart
February 2010

Serving Undergraduate and Graduate Students,
Faculty, Staff, Community

Core Services & Products

Research Support Services Team (RSST)	Instructional Services Team (IST)	Access & Information Services Team (AIST)	Document Delivery Team (DDT)	Center for Creative Photography (CCP)	Special Collections (SC)

Infrastructure Services

Digital Library Information Systems Team (DLIST)	Library Support Services Team (LSST)	Technical Services Team (TST)

Administrative & Governance Services

Governance: LFA Library Faculty Assembly	SLRP/BAG Strategic Long-Range Planning Team & Budget Advisory Group	PMG Portfolio Management Group	MROC Millennium Report Oversight Committee	TAC Technology Architecture Council	IAMO Information Access Management Oversight	Governance: SGA Staff Governance Association

Library Cabinet
Functional Team Leaders + Dean + Associate Dean + Assistant Dean + LFA and SGA representatives

Library Administration
Dean, Associate Dean, Assistant Dean for Technology Strategy, Director of Project Management & Assessment, Director of Development, Director of Copyright Management & Scholarly Communication, and Special Collections

Fig. 1 University of Arizona libraries organization chart.

Therefore, four functional domains were created: Connection Development, Education, Information Resources Management, and Content Management.

This changed how members of RSST communicated with faculty and students. Losing direct connection with departments through the liaison model created issues and concerns about the most effective way for RSST to conduct needs assessments.

Each year, as part of the review of the Libraries' strategic plan, the Strategic Long-Range Planning Team (SLRP) recommended the year's critical few projects, partly based on an environmental scan of new information and trends on campus. In 2010 SLRP noted that,

A steady reduction in our personnel resources as librarian lines have been lost to budget cuts has meant that we are no longer approaching liaison work in traditional ways. Nonetheless, we still need to provide effective research resources and assistance to faculty and other researchers at the University. In addition, new opportunities have arisen for the Libraries to demonstrate our value to the University. (University of Arizona Libraries, Strategic Long-Range Planning Team, p. 2)

SLRP challenged the Libraries to work with faculty in new and different ways, and to build relationships to support research and grant activities. These activities included:

- Involvement at the outset of research projects and grant activities, specifically through data management and institutional repository services.
- Providing enhanced information resources and research assistance.

The latter included, but was not limited to, expanding librarians' interactions with faculty and researchers in order to better understand their research needs.

A. Developing Research and Grant Support Services

As a result of SLRP's challenge and the recent restructuring changes, a project was defined in October 2010 with a goal to:

Explore ways to become effective at increasing research and grant support to faculty, researchers, and graduate students in a scalable way, to help the campus increase achievements in research, scholarship, and creative works. This project will better define the Libraries' role in research and grant support, determine the optimal points in the research and grant cycles for the Library to be involved, and explore ways to be involved at these points. (University of Arizona Libraries, Research Support Services Team, p. 1)

A project definition document was developed as part of the Libraries' project management process. The document included assumptions, the purpose and objectives of the project, scope, project deliverables, and who would be involved such as project sponsor, project manager, project member, and stakeholders. The project team consisted of the RSST Team Leader as the project's sponsor, and two RSST team members, one who served as project manager and the other as a project member. As the project progressed, other RSST members volunteered to assist the project team. The process involved a review of the literature, interviews with UAL's peer libraries, university department heads and the campus units involved in research and grant activities, and a survey of graduate and professional students. At different points in the project, various library stakeholders were asked for feedback. When each deliverable was completed, it was shared with library staff. The project deliverables included the following:

- Develop baseline of current UAL research and grant support services;
- Benchmark research and grant support services that are provided by UAL's peer and other libraries (such as Pac-10 institutions not considered UAL peers);
- Develop a definition of research and grant support services;

- Determine research and grant support needs on campus and examine a variety of research and grant cycle models;
- Develop recommendations and strategies for providing more comprehensive and systematic support for research and grant activities on campus, determine where in the research cycle the Libraries should be involved, establish connections with campus stakeholders, and develop strategies for increasing Library support including measures for these services; and
- Develop marketing strategies to promote new research and grant support services.

II. Methodology

After the definition document was completed and approved by the RSST Team Leader (project's sponsor), the tasks were determined that needed to be accomplished to achieve the project's purpose, objectives, and deliverables. Additionally, who would be assigned tasks and deadlines was decided. This enabled development of a plan for identifying existing research and grant support services to be offered in the future. The work conducted during this phase was accomplished from October 2010 to June 2011.

A. Baseline of Existing UAL Services

In order to baseline what the UAL currently offered, different methods were used. A review of UAL's web site yielded a draft list of five major services: the Campus Repository Service, inter-library loan services (ILL), in-depth reference, geospatial data and GIS software help, and copyright and scholarly communication. The draft list was sent to library staff to identify gaps. The final list comprised 10 services (see Appendix A) which UAL provided in support of research and grant activities.

B. Literature Review, Peer Practices, and Internal Assessments

A literature review was undertaken to identify services provided by other libraries which UAL could potentially provide. In library literature data-bases, 30 articles and 6 monographs on research and grant support services were identified. As the project team reviewed the literature, the following questions were asked:

1. What other research and grant services were libraries providing?
2. How did they implement research and grant services? What level of staff/number of staff did they have for the service?
3. What did they include under research and grant support services? (This helped with a later deliverable, namely defining research support services and grant support services.)
4. What was the relationship of the library organization to research and grant support services?

5. Did the article provide information from faculty and students perspectives about the effectiveness of services?
6. Whom did they serve?

The articles reviewed fell into broad themes—data management, grant support, e-Research, and research support. Several articles and reports covered data management. Soehner, Steeves, and Ward (2010) made the following general observations:

- Collaborations are essential to address even modest support of e-Science;
- Faculty interest and institutional support at the administrative level are important for success of library services in this area;
- Master of Library and Information Science degree has a place in this new area of librarianship;
- Support for research and grant activities is a priority for libraries (investments are being made during difficult budget times);
- Strategies for data curation, management, and preservation are still young and evolving.

The report included examples of several libraries that had instituted data support services.

Brandt (2007) wrote about librarians as key partners in e-Research. He noted that faculty need the knowledge that librarians have such as the ability to collect, organize, describe, curate, archive, and disseminate data and information. Means (2000) wrote about a joint venture developed between the University of Washington Health Sciences Library and Information Center and the School of Medicine to provide in-depth service in grant funding and grant acquisitions skills. Other articles fell under the categories of e-Research or research support. Luce (2008) stated that, "Librarians and informaticians must be involved in the early planning and data-modeling phases of e-Research to ensure the collection, preservation, ease of use, and availability of data today and in the future" (p. 44). He asserted that "librarians must become part of the research process—full members of the research team. To do this, library staff members need to 'go native' and embed themselves among the teams they support" (p. 48). Case (2008) provided examples of several types of services that libraries can provide: help with metadata structures and controlled vocabularies, copyright issues, preservation solutions, digitization services, digital repositories, and publishing. Case states that "... librarians bring a set of values that are fundamental to the long-term survival of scholarship" (p. 144). Borchert and Young (2010) in an article about Queensland University of Technology (QUT), provided their definition of research support as "the provision of information resources and discovery services, bibliographic management software, assistance with publishing (publishing strategies, identifying high impact journals, dealing with publishers and the peer review process), citation analysis and calculating authors' H Index" (p. 2). They reported that QUT Libraries would be collaborating with the campus information technology department to provide research data management services and that they would teach a course for Ph.D. students on advanced information retrieval.

1. Peer Practices

To go beyond the literature review and learn about unique services other academic libraries were providing, 40 library web sites were identified from UAL peers, libraries at Pac-10 institutions, and recommendations from the project stakeholders. Of the 40, 10 were found to offer research and grant support services which UAL did not provide.

Given the limited information found from the literature and web site reviews, it became apparent that interviews would be needed and 19 libraries were identified to interview for additional information.

In addition to the two RSST librarians on the project team, three additional librarians from the RSST volunteered to help with interviews. A variety of methods were used for the interviews—in-person, Skype, and telephone. The following questions were asked:

1. Who do you serve?
2. What services do you provide related to research and grant support?
3. Do you have an organizational chart that you can share with us that shows how the department is structured?
4. How much staff and budget do you allocate to these services?
5. At what point in the research cycle is the library involved?
6. Do you have established connections with campus units/departments involved with research and grant support?
7. How do you market your services?
8. How much use do the services get?

The majority (11 out of 19) of libraries interviewed served primarily faculty, graduate students, and staff. Some also worked with students in general (both undergraduates and graduate students). The services provided were grouped in four major areas—data services, scholarly communication, research services, and grant support. Data services included providing data management consulting services for faculty, storage and backup services, metadata services, data analysis, formatting of data, data publishing, and digitizing. Many libraries began focusing on data management after the National Science Foundation instituted a requirement (in January 2011) that all grant proposals must include a data management plan. Scholarly communication included providing copyright and open access publishing information and author rights workshops. Research services included various research skills workshops and in-depth reference. Grant support included reviewing preliminary grant proposals, grant services, and serving as co-principal investigators.

Since UAL sought to provide scalable research and grant support services, information was needed about how many staff were devoted to these activities and how the libraries were organized. There was a range in how these services were provided. Some had separate units with two to four staff devoted to research and grant support, but also relying on liaison librarians who devote part of their time to research and grant support. Others had a coordinator for the service and liaison librarians who devoted part of their time to this work. Some research and grant support services such as data management had recently been implemented, so the libraries were not certain how much use that service would get. Other libraries reported seeing high use from recently implemented services and knew that they needed additional staff to deal with demands.

Part of the project team's charge was to explore where in a research cycle the libraries should be involved. Again the majority (11 of 19) of respondents said they were involved throughout the entire research cycle. A few said they were mainly involved at the beginning and at the end of research cycles, and not as much in the middle stages. Since research and grant support services could be provided by other units on campus, interviewees were asked with what campus units their libraries had established connections. Thirteen of 19 respondents said they had established connections with the vice president for research or with academic departments through liaison librarians. Others mentioned they had established connections with campus information technology departments and units that dealt with sponsored projects.

When asked how libraries marketed their services, most respondents indicated that marketing was done through librarian liaisons by attending various campus meetings, or through a wide range of marketing tools. Two indicated that they marketed their services through the vice president for research.

2. Defining Research and Grant Support Services

One of the deliverables of the project was to create clearly defined definitions of research and grant support. The project group developed a draft, requested feedback from library staff, and based on the feedback, finalized a definition (see Appendix B). The definition was also used in the campus needs assessment interviews.

After developing a definition of research and grant support, determining campus research and grant support needs was necessary. This was accomplished by interviewing department, individuals providing research and grant support services, and a survey of graduate and professional students.

3. Department Head Interviews

Another RSST project, Increasing Campus Connections, had planned to meet with university department heads to communicate services and resources provided by the UAL and to ask them about new, desired resources and services. The Research and Grant Support Services project team had also planned to interview department heads. Therefore the RGSS project team asked the Increasing Campus Connections project if they would be willing to add questions to their interview schedule. It was agreed that the following questions be added:

1. Are there additional services related to research or grant support the library could provide for you, faculty, researchers, or graduate students in your department?
2. Since the National Science Foundation and the National Institute of Health are requiring researchers who are submitting grant proposals to submit a data management plan or data sharing plan, how can the library help?

Increasing Campus Connections identified 47 department heads from 10 colleges to contact. Only 21 department heads (representing 10 colleges) were available to meet face-to-face and give input.

Ten out of 21 department heads saw a clear role for UAL related to research and grant support. Some of the responses [number of mentions] included:

- Help with developing data management plans, although they had questions about what services the libraries would provide [7]
- Help with the submission process for certain grants (e.g., help obtaining permission from publishers as part of the grant submission process) [4]
- Alerting service for grant opportunities [3]
- Help to develop databases (part of a research project) [2]
- Help with setting up database systems so that the data could be easily de-identified for purposes of data sharing [1]
- One department suggested that in order to offer data management services, the libraries would need the right technical staff, offer a competitive cost, and storage options need to be in place when data management plans are being written [1]
- Any solution to long-term storage or accessibility of very large data files [1]
- Literature reviews for grant proposals [1]
- Provide guidance to graduate students on doing citation analysis [1]

4. Individual Interviews

Individuals who provided research or grant support services at UA's college, departmental, or unit levels were identified through web sites and recommendations by library staff. Ten such individuals were interviewed individually, face-to-face and asked the following questions:

1. What services do you offer? Are grant consultations, grantsmanship workshops, and grant proposal writing workshops offered on a regular basis? Can the library help with grantsmanship or grant proposal writing workshops? What demand do you have for grant consultations? Can the library help with grant consultations?

2. What are your plans for helping faculty and students with data management plans, will you be offering workshops? (As background for this question, interviewees were provided with information about the library's and campus plans for supporting data management such as campus presentations, the designation of one FTE librarian for data management, and establishment of a Campus Data Management and Curation Advisory Committee to look at how the campus can support faculty and researchers).

3. How can we collaborate? Are you interested in collaborating on grant workshops and data management workshops?

4. Do they know of other people to whom we should talk?

There was a wide range of grant support provided to individual faculty, depending on the department or school. Support for grant proposals was provided at college and department levels. Two colleges provided a grant alerting service, some offered grantsmanship workshops for faculty, while others had faculty with experience at various granting agencies helping others to prepare grants. Two out of the 10 people interviewed indicated that their college provided limited support.

Three of the 10 interviewees were interested in collaborating. They suggested that the Libraries coordinate grantsmanship workshops and develop workshop modules on topics such as literature reviews and data management. One person thought it was important for the Libraries to develop and maintain a database of UA researchers that would include the researcher's area of research and the granting agencies to which they had applied in order to form a networking resource for faculty.

5. Student Surveys

Graduate and professional students were identified as an important customer group from whom to obtain feedback from on research and grant services. In fiscal year 2009/2010, there were 8494 graduate and professional students at the UA. They were served by the UA Graduate and Professional Student Council (GPSC), which had 31 college level representatives. The

GPSC representatives were approached with a proposal to conduct an online survey. The representatives distributed surveys by e-mail lists to graduate and professional students in their colleges during a one-month period in the spring semester of 2011. It is unclear how many e-mails were sent and how many surveys were distributed. Survey questions were as follows:

1. Please indicate your University of Arizona affiliation.
2. What department(s) or unit(s) are you affiliated with?
3. What additional services related to research or grant support could the Library provide for graduate and professional students?
4. Are you working on specific projects that would benefit from research and grant support from the Library?
5. If yes, please tell us about the project and how the library could help.
6. Are you a graduate research assistant?
7. If yes, is there specific research or grant support the library could provide for you and the faculty member you work for?
8. National Science Foundation and the National Institute of Health are requiring researchers submitting grants to submit a data management or data sharing plans. How can the Library support you as you are developing these plans?
9. May we contact you for follow-up questions?

The RGSS project team received responses from 259 (3.07%) graduate and professional students. Table 1 provides details about the survey participants' college affiliation and type of student.

Responses clustered into several themes: grant and grant support services, research workshops, data management plans, and scholarly communication. As mentioned in interviews with individuals providing campus research and grant support, many graduate and professional students needed help with finding grant sources and writing proposals. Several suggested that the Libraries offer grantsmanship workshops, including grant writing and grant application services. There were also several suggestions that the Libraries provide an alerting service for grants by discipline and develop a database of previous grants. The number of students suggesting the Libraries provide grant and grant support services is summarized in Table 2.

Graduate students also suggested that the Libraries provide workshops on a variety of topics such as the research process, research writing, how and where to get published, copyright issues, managing references, citation analysis, and literature searches. The number of graduate and professional students who suggested the Libraries offer workshops is provided in Table 3.

Table 1
Graduate and Professional Student Survey Respondents

College affiliation	Number of respondents	Percent	Graduate students	Professional Students
Social and Behavioral Sciences	133	51.3	132	1
Science	52	20.1	52	0
Optical Sciences	1	0.4	1	0
Agricultural and Life Sciences	5	1.9	5	0
Engineering	1	0.4	1	0
Education	1	0.4	1	0
Business Management	8	3.1	8	0
Law	2	0.8	0	2
Humanities	4	1.5	4	0
Medicine	22	8.5	5	17
Public Health	16	6.2	16	0
Graduate Inter-Disciplinary Programs (GIDPs)	6	2.3	6	0
Not indicated	8	3.1	8	0
Total	259	100.0	239	20

Table 2
Grant and Grant Support Services

College affiliation	Number of respondents	Graduate students
Social and Behavioral Sciences	10	10
Science	5	5
Agricultural and Life Sciences	1	1
Business Management	1	1
Public Health	4	4
GIDPs	1	1
Total	22	22

Table 3
Workshops

College affiliation	Number of respondents	Graduate students	Professional students
Social and Behavioral Sciences	14	14	0
Science	1	1	0
Medicine	2	0	2
Public Health	2	2	0
Not indicated	2	2	0
Total	21	19	2

The category that received the most feedback was on data management, and came from respondents in the Colleges of Science, Social and Behavioral Sciences, and Engineering. Comments fell into the following categories:

• Data management and data sharing workshops or tutorials (how to write a plan, data management tools and techniques, what data needs to be shared);
• Examples of data management plans;
• Generic data management plans or templates;
• Storage of data (public access or campus only);
• Access to sensitive data (confidential or restricted access);
• Storage of large datasets;
• Collaborative space for researchers;
• Consulting with someone who would provide feedback on a draft plan;
• Guidance to graduate students on intellectual property rights and access rights;
• Help with submission of data to specific repositories.

The number of students suggesting that the Libraries provide data management services is summarized in Table 4.

III. Data Analyses

The data were analyzed by reviewing all the responses from the benchmarking, campus needs assessment, and graduate and professional student surveys. The project team reviewed the interview notes, answers to survey questions, and comments or suggestions. Each comment and suggestion was coded, and organized under themes or concepts. The students' survey results were more complicated to analyze due to the larger number of responses.

Table 4
Data Management

College affiliation	Number of respondents	Graduate students
Social and Behavioral Sciences	35	35
Science	10	10
Public Health	3	3
GIDPs	1	1
Not indicated	1	1
Total	50	50

After the results of the benchmarking and campus needs assessment were coded and categorized, all results were integrated into one analysis (see Appendix C). This overall data analysis provided the framework for developing the final recommendations for new research and grant support services by the libraries. The data analyses were conducted from June to July 2011.

IV. Results

When recommendations were in draft form, they were discussed with the leaders of the teams which would be responsible for implementing the recommendations. After receiving e-mail feedback from library staff, recommendations were finalized and all of the deliverables were shared with library staff via e-mail. Final recommendations and strategies developed as of October 2011 are given below, listing first the recommendations and then the strategies for implementation.

A. Recommendations and Strategies

1. Data Management

It was recommended that the UAL develop a data management service. This recommendation was based on campus needs, NSF, and other federal agencies mandates, and what is being increasingly seen in the literature as the future work of libraries. In addition, many peer libraries were currently offering this service. It will provide a central point for data management and data curation on campus in support of the beginning, middle, and end stages of the research process. It was also recommended that UAL develop a web site and training sessions to assist with data management. The following approaches were suggested:

- Develop a definition of what the library is trying to accomplish;
- Develop a web site to provide faculty a central point of information as they are developing data management plans, initially focusing on NSF and NIH data management plan requirements;
- Develop faculty and researcher training sessions on how to write data management plans;
- Develop an organizational model for scaling out the Libraries' support of data management;
- Develop a marketing plan to promote the Libraries' data management support services; and
- Participate in the Association of Research Libraries (ARL)/Digital Library Federation (DLF) E-Science Institute to help develop a strategic agenda for e-Science support.

2. Grants

The RGSS project team recommended that UAL develop grant support services to be offered to campus. Since there was uneven support for identifying grant sources, the project group saw an opportunity for the library to play a pivotal role as a central location for grant information and for support at the beginning stage of the research process. The following approaches were recommended:

- Continue subscribing to the *Illinois Researcher Information Service* to support grant activities;
- Include the following on the Research and Grant Support webpage:
  - ○ Links to the UA Foundations' Grant Information, Facilitation and Training Center, including the Grants for Lunch program;
  - ○ Organize grant funding opportunities by discipline;
  - ○ Link to the AzGates web site which provides information about grant opportunities based on user-defined profiled; and
- Consider collaborating with other campus units that provide grant services and workshops.

3. Database for Researchers

The RGSS project recommended that UAL develop a database for researchers to consult as they develop grant proposals, and use as a resource to reach other researchers for advice and potential collaboration.

Two potential alternatives were identified for developing an in-house database. Both alternatives needed to be investigated in further depth.

- Consider utilizing the campus database for tracking grants via Sponsored Projects, currently being revised and updated, along with other campus computer systems. When in place, this database will make it possible to search by Principal Investigator, keywords in titles, grant amount, and the status of applications—submitted, pending, awarded, renewed, etc.

- Consider setting up a subscription to the *Community of Science Expertise* database. Faculty members would need to input their data in the database and update as needed. The Libraries would need to examine subscription costs and the likelihood that faculty and researchers would contribute information into the database.

4. Metadata

The RGSS team recommended that UAL develop metadata services to be offered for faculty and graduate students to accomplish their research and collect findings more efficiently and effectively. The Campus Data Management and Curation Advisory Committee had identified this as a service the Library could provide throughout all research stages. The RGSS project team suggested the following metadata services:

- Consultations about metadata schema to use for organizing data;
- Consultations on the indexing terms to use (approved names, such as MeSH); and
- How to make the data searchable.

5. Training

The RGSS project recommended that the Libraries develop specific training sessions. The types of training needs mentioned by faculty and students were how to do effective and efficient research, scholarly communication resources, citation management, and citation analysis. It was recommended that these could be met with online tutorials, videos, or by individual assistance throughout all research stages.

6. Research and Grant Support Webpage

The RGSS project recommended that the Libraries develop an overall Research and Grant Support webpage as a central location for people to go for information on research and grant support, including information about grants, training sessions offered by the UAL, links to the Data Management web site and to relevant campus units and services.

7. Collaborative Tools

The RGSS project recommended that the Libraries provide server space where research teams could share data while working on a project.

8. Marketing Plan

The final deliverable for the project was to develop a marketing plan for library teams to use in implementing project recommendations. The project team developed ideas for UAL to promote new research and grant support services, as follows:

- Send messages to various campus e-mail lists;
- List on campus calendars any workshops developed collaboratively with other units;
- Include articles in newsletter to campus or campus groups;
- Develop press releases (3-D memos) that are sent to campus;
- Hold an open house of new research and grant support services offered by the Libraries;
- Promote new services to campus groups by relevant library teams;
- Announce new services on UAL's web site;
- Use direct marketing to targeted individuals or groups such as:
  - Vice President for Research;
  - Graduate College;
  - Deans and Directors of Colleges;
  - Graduate Student and Professional Student Council;
  - New faculty and new students at orientations;
  - Campus advisory groups and committees; and
  - Faculty at departmental and other meetings.

It was also suggested that the Dean of the Libraries sends e-mail to other Deans about new library services; and that announcements and brochures be distributed at relevant symposia and colloquia.

B. Progress Toward Implementation

1. Data Management

UAL made progress in implementing the data management recommendations since it became one of the critical few goals for fiscal year 2010/2011. The Campus Data Management and Curation Advisory Committee, co-chaired by faculty members from the UAL and the Office of Vice President for Research (VPR), was appointed early in 2011. This Committee developed recommendations that were shared with the UAL Dean and the VPR. The Committee met with the UAL Dean and VPR in February 2012 to discuss the Committee's recommendations.

In May 2011, UAL appointed one FTE as Data Curation Librarian to provide support toward development of data management services on campus. Since being appointed this Librarian developed a Data Management web site to provide information on developing data management plans.

Co-chairs of the Campus Data Management and Curation Advisory Committee and the Data Curation Librarian had begun to participate in the ARL/DLF E-Science Institute as of the final draft of this chapter.

In addition, the Libraries developed a library-wide data management goal for fiscal year 2011/2012. The objective was to develop a data management strategy which addressed current and long-term data management needs on campus related to granting agencies' requirements. This was to include recommendations on services the UAL will provide, recommendations on an organizational model for scaling out support for data management, and a strategy for developing data curation expertise in the Library. It is expected that the e-Science strategic agenda developed from participating in the E-Science Institute will inform the work of this project team.

2. Grants

This recommendation has been designated as a project placeholder for fiscal year 2011/2012 based on human resources. During the spring semester, this project placeholder may be developed into full-fledged project if the Libraries determine that there is sufficient human resources to devote to this project.

3. Database for Researchers

This recommendation has been designated as a project placeholder for fiscal year 2011/2012. During the spring semester, this project placeholder may be developed into full-fledged project if the Libraries determine that there is sufficient human resources to devote to this project.

4. Metadata

Currently, faculty consult with the Campus Repository Manager on the appropriate metadata schema to use for their collection in the campus repository. This fiscal year (2011/2012), the Libraries are working on a project to develop an internal metadata workflow and to determine in-house costs for developing metadata records.

5. Training

The Libraries developed and taught a one-credit Graduate Student Research class in fall 2011, to be taught again in spring 2012. This class was developed to address the majority of research needs of graduate students.

6. Research and Grant Support Webpage

This recommendation has been designated as a project placeholder for fiscal year 2011/2012. During the spring semester, this project placeholder may be developed into full-fledged project if the Libraries determine that there are sufficient human resources to devote to this project.

7. Collaborative Tools

University Information Technology Services does not currently offer such services, but is considering adding it to the computing services and resources that they offer.

8. Marketing

When new research and grant support services are developed by the Libraries, the marketing strategies recommended will be implemented.

V. Limitations

The RGSS project team experienced limitations that affected the project. A major limitation was the short time frame the project team had to make recommendations. The campus needs assessment had to be completed during the spring semester of 2011. Because GPSC college representatives were responsible for sending out the students' survey, the number of surveys distributed was not known. If there had been more time, RGSS could have used different methods, such as direct surveys and focus groups, to obtain more data. In addition, the Increasing Campus Connections project encountered time limitations in collecting data, since it also needed to finish departments' head interviews by the end of spring semester 2011.

Another limitation was the lack of librarians to help with the project. If more librarians had been available to help with needs assessment, the project may have been able to obtain more input from campus customers.

The project team was also limited by the amount of input it received from library staff. While helpful recommendations from RSST colleagues were received throughout the project general library staff provided little feedback. The reason for lack of response could have been that the project lacked relevance to their immediate responsibilities.

Despite the short time frame, limited feedback from faculty, graduate and professional students, research and grant support units, and general library staff, the RGSS team was able to obtain enough information to propose recommendations about needed research and grant support services.

VI. Conclusion

The chapter has given a basic framework for libraries to use when conducting needs assessment. Although it presented one specific library's example, the methodology gives insights into how to successfully develop a baseline, review external peers, and conduct campus needs assessment. The recommendations provide examples of potential new research and grant support services that libraries could offer. The chapter also provides a rationale for why the UAL conducted needs assessment for research and grant support and shows how the results of needs assessment can be used for strategic planning and be incorporated into library operations and projects.

With all the changes that libraries and universities are facing, libraries need to have a good understanding of customer needs. New library services and resources need to be developed in collaboration with, or at least with substantial feedback from stakeholders such as faculty, staff, and students. This makes effective needs assessment of campus communities important and something in need of increasing attention in the coming years.

Acknowledgments

The authors would like to acknowledge the assistance of Jim Martin, Jennalyn Tellman, and Raik Zaghloul in interviewing other libraries.

Appendix A: Research and Grant Support Activities and Services (December 2010)

Scholarly Communication

- Help researchers sort out copyright questions for their use of third party material and for how they want their own material used.
- Help create and promote more open environments for sharing and communicating research results.
- Support for online projects such as open access like journals.

Information Resource Management

- Resources, evaluation, and selection.

Grants

- Librarians served as Co-PIs on grants.
- Librarians provided literature reviews for grants.
- Librarians advised on portal technology requirements and metadata schema design.
- Libraries wrote sections of grants related to data management plans.
- Librarians wrote library collection sections for title VI grants.

Repository

- Campus Repository Service—service for faculty/graduate students to organize their research; expands access to research and spurs additional research.

Datasets

- Host datasets.
- Currently exploring possibilities for library role in dataset publication/storage for UA faculty.
- Work with faculty to provide open access to data generated in research study.

Collaborating

- Collaborate across multiple institutions.
- Partner with faculty on digital projects to identify resources and other material useful to students and researchers.

Reference

- Teach effective literature review strategies to graduate students.
- Locate information related to research project.

- In-depth reference (related to research, not class assignments)—service to help faculty and graduate students how to find the information they need and where to find it such as:
  - Teach graduate students how to do research
  - Literature review for theses/dissertations
- Find geospatial data and how to use GIS software—service to help faculty and graduate students find the information they need and where to find it; any data conversions that are needed and how to use ArcGIS software.
- Provide citation counts about research to specific faculty or departments.
- Provide data for accreditation and academic program reviews.
- Provide library and information resources data for new degree.
- Help graduate students format their dissertation.

ILL

- Provide access to research materials outside of the library.

Communication

- Promote and instruct UA community on using databases.
- Online orientation tutorials for graduate students and face-to-face orientations.

Instruction

- Upcoming—Graduate 1 credit course on library research focused on complementary departments or colleges.

Appendix B: Research and Grant Support Definition

The purpose of Research and Grant Support Services is to provide in-depth information support to faculty, students, and researchers at the University of Arizona. The primary goal is to help faculty, students, and researchers be more productive in their research projects and programs. These services provide support to research in all disciplines at various points in the research cycle. The services provided are complimentary and do not duplicate research and grant support services that other campus units provide.
Some examples of this work include

Advanced Reference:

- Research assistance for faculty, students, and researchers in all areas including data.
- Train research assistants on how to effectively find relevant information for faculty.
- Train faculty and researchers on how to effectively find relevant information.
- Grant activities (include grant searching and alert services).

Data Management

- Data curation service—data curation is the active and ongoing management of data through its lifecycle of interest and usefulness [defining longevity of the data] to scholarship, science, and education. Data curation activities enable data discovery and retrieval, maintain its quality, add value, and provide for reuse over time, and this new field includes authentication, archiving, management, preservation, retrieval, and representation (UIUC Data Curation Education Program at the University of Illinois Urbana-Champaign, http://cirss.lis.illinois.edu/CollMeta/dcep.html).
- Data management plans—a data management plan is a formal document that outlines what you will do with your data during and after you complete your research. We find that most researchers have some form of a data management plan, but often don't know the full scope of issues to sort out or perhaps plan to figure it out later (University of Virginia Library Scientific Data Consulting, http://www2.lib.virginia.edu/brown/data/plan.html). For example the University of Virginia Library serves as a consultant for the following:
  - Organizing Files and File Formats
  - Security, Storage and Backups
  - Funding Guidelines
  - Copyright and Privacy/Confidentiality of Data
  - Data Documentation and Metadata
  - Archiving and Sharing Data
  - Citing Data
- Provide metadata (consultative)—for example help faculty or students decide what metadata schema to use

Campus Repository Service

- Host research methods and outputs, creative works, publications, and teaching materials to further the pursuit of discovery and learning to all.

Scholarly Communication

- Publishing venues (consultation on possible publishing venues, including open access journals).
- Copyright issues, work they want to use, and their own material (e.g., Creative Commons).
- Develop guides to help faculty etc. negotiate with publishers.

Citation Analysis

- Show impact of research or publication to individual, department, or college (providing the information or training).
- Impact factors of journals.

Miscellaneous

- Online and physical collaborative spaces.
- Lab for digital projects, where there are librarians and other experts available (such as UVA's Scholars Lab).

- Database of researchers.
- Variety of workshops on topics such as NSF Data Management requirements, Increasing Your Impact and Retaining Your Rights, and Impact Factor.

Appendix C: Research and Grant Support Services Final Data Analysis

The final analysis consists of major areas that came out of the compiled results from interviews with other libraries and campus contacts, increasing campus connections project, and the graduate and professional students' survey.

Data Management

Results from interviews with other libraries
Ten out of 19 libraries interviewed had some type of data management service or were planning to have data management services in the near future. The type of work included help with data management plans, digital humanities, data management workshops, and data management consultations.

Campus contacts/Individual interviews
Four out of 10 people interviewed saw a role for the library in providing data management services. Specifically what was mentioned was helping customers with data management plan support and being interested in collaborating with the library on workshops or training sessions around data management.

Graduate and professional students survey
Fifty out of 259 graduate and professional students indicated a need for data management support. More specifically the type of services they were looking for were: data management and data sharing workshops or tutorials (how to write a plan, data management tools and techniques, what data needs to be shared), examples of data management plans, generic data management plans or templates, storage of data (public access or campus only), access to sensitive data (confidential or restricted access), storage of large datasets, collaborative space for researchers, consulting with someone who would cross-check a draft plan, guidance to graduate students on intellectual property rights and access rights, help with submission of data to specific repositories. For example, in the results of the graduate and professional students' survey, a graduate student expressed a need for help with submission and formatting of NCBI's large-scale sequencing data.

Increasing campus connections project
Seven out of 21 department heads interviewed saw a role for the library related to data management. There was interest expressed in librarians being available to help organize data, develop data management plans, develop databases (part of a research project), and set up database systems so that the data could be easily de-identified for purposes of data sharing. In addition, some had questions about what services the libraries would provide.

Grants

Results from interviews with other libraries
Four out of 19 libraries interviewed had some type of grant support that they offered to their campus. The type of work included one-on-one grant consultations to identify funding opportunities, grant workshops, and e-mail grant alerts.

Campus contacts/Individual interviews
Four out of 10 people interviewed saw a role for the library related to grant support. Specifically what was mentioned was help identifying funding opportunities, conducting grant searching workshops, and collaborating with them to see what further grant support could be offered by the library.

Graduate and professional students survey
Twenty-two out of 259 graduate and professional students indicated they would like the library to offer grant support services. Specifically they need help finding and writing grant proposals. The students also suggested that the Libraries offer grantsmanship workshops, including grant writing and grant application services. There were also several suggestions for the Libraries to provide an alerting service on what grants are available by discipline and to develop a database of previous grants.

Increasing campus connections project
Seven out of 21 department heads saw a role for the library in relation to grant support. The kind of support mentioned were: help with the sub-mission process for certain grants (e.g., help obtaining permission from publishers as part of the grant submission process), alerting service for grant opportunities, literature reviews for grant proposals, and help with process for submission of grant proposals to NIH (requesting permission from each publisher, since NIH requires that the article is also published in PubMed Central).

Database of Researchers

Results from interviews with other libraries
Nothing was mentioned during the interviews about a database of researchers.

Campus contacts/Individual interviews
One out of 10 people mentioned the library could help compile and maintain a database of researchers to increase collaboration on campus and to keep an inventory of researchers with grant writing experience for specific grants.

Graduate and professional students survey
Two out of 259 of the graduate students suggested that it would be useful if the Libraries developed a database of previous grant proposals by graduate students and faculty.

Increasing campus connections project
This was not mentioned in the interviews with department heads.

Metadata (Data Management and Campus Repository Service)

Results from interviews with other libraries
Six out of 19 libraries interviewed offered metadata services. The type of work included help identifying metadata standard/schema or data standard, help researchers be consistent in data creation and metadata, fee-based metadata services to provide assistance with digital production projects at the university, and help providing metadata for documentation of data.

Campus contacts/Individual interviews
Nothing was mentioned during the interviews about metadata services.

Graduate and professional students survey
This did not come up in the survey results.

Increasing campus connections project
This did not come up during the interviews.

Training Sessions (in Addition to Data Management and Grantsmanship Training Sessions)

Results from interviews with other libraries
All (19 out of 19) of the libraries interviewed offer some form of training sessions. The types of training sessions included copyright and scholarly

communication, research help, information literacy, author rights, and subject-specific research help.

Campus contacts/Individual interviews
Four out of 10 people interviewed thought that training sessions offered by the library would be useful for customers. Sessions mentioned were data management plans, grant support, and research support.

Graduate and professional students survey
Twenty-one out of 259 graduate and professional students suggested that the Libraries provide workshops on a variety of topics. Some of the suggestions included workshops on the research process, research writing, how and where to get published, copyright issues, managing references, citation analysis, and literature searches.

Increasing campus connections project
Three out of 21 department heads mentioned training sessions and how they would be useful for graduate students. It was stated how helpful the training sessions would be to their research and accomplishing their research. The following types of sessions were mentioned: research skills, grant seeking, and providing guidance to graduate students on doing citation analysis.

Research and Grant Support Webpage

Results from interviews with other libraries
Ten out 19 libraries had some form of a web site to promote their research and grant support services and activities. Information on their web sites included information about tutorials, training sessions, links to grant help, and how to contact a librarian for consultations on research or data management.

Campus contacts/Individual interviews
One out of 10 people mentioned that it would be useful for the library to maintain a central web site for customers to be able to go to for information about research and grant support on campus.

Graduate and professional students survey
This did not come up in the survey results.

Increasing campus connections project
This was not mentioned during the interviews with department heads.

Collaboration Tools

Results from interviews other libraries
One of the 19 libraries offered a space for faculty to collaborate online.

Campus contacts/Individual interviews
This did not come up during the interviews.

Graduate and professional students survey
Two out of 259 graduate students suggested that campus provide access to a secure server that researchers could use to share data with other project members.

Increasing campus connections project
One out of 21 department heads mentioned it would be very useful for the library to have an online collaboration tool to share project data with other project members both on-campus and at other universities.

References

Borchert, M., & Young, J. (2010, June). Coordinated research support services at Queensland University of Technology, Australia. Paper presented at the 31st Annual Conference of the International Association of Scientific and Technological University Libraries, West Lafayette, IN and Chicago, IL. Retrieved from http://docs.lib.purdue.edu/cgi/viewcontent.cgi?article=1008&context=iatul2010

Brandt, D. S. (2007). Librarians as partners in e-Research: Purdue Universities promote collaboration. *College & Research Libraries News*, 68(6), 365–367, 396. Retrieved from http://crln.acrl.org/content/68/6/365.full.pdf

Case, M. M. (2008). Partners in knowledge creation: An expanded role for research libraries in the digital future. *Journal of Library Administration*, 48(2), 141–156. doi:10.1080/01930820802231336

Luce, R. E. (2008). A new value equation challenge: The emergence of eResearch and roles for research libraries. In *No brief candle: Reconceiving research libraries for the 21st century* (pp. 42–50). Washington, DC: Council on Library and Information Resources. Retrieved from http://www.clir.org/pubs/reports/pub142/pub142.pdf

Means, M. L. (2000). The research funding service: A model for expanded library services. *Bulletin of the Medical Library Association*, 88(2), 178–186. Retrieved from http://www.ncbi.nlm.nih.gov/pmc/articles/PMC35218/pdf/i0025-7338-088-02-0178.pdf

Soehner, C., Steeves, C., & Ward, J. (2010). *E-Science and data support services: A study of ARL member institutions*. Washington, DC: Association of Research Libraries. Retrieved from http://www.arl.org/bm~doc/escience_report2010.pdf

University of Arizona Libraries. (2007). *2007 Restructuring team charge*. Unpublished report. Tucson, AZ: Author.

University of Arizona Libraries, Restructuring Team. (2008). *New organizational structure: Teams and roles*. Unpublished report. Tucson, AZ: Author.

University of Arizona Libraries, Research Support Services Team. (2010a). *Project definition document: Research and grant support services*. Unpublished report. Tucson, AZ: Author.

University of Arizona Libraries, Strategic Long-Range Planning Team. (2010b). *Recommended critical few for FY 2010–2011*. Tucson, AZ: Author. Retrieved from http://intranet.library.arizona.edu/xf/slrp/pandp.html

The Relationship between Collection Strength and Student Achievement

Rachel Wexelbaum[a] and Mark A. Kille[b]
[a]Department of Information Media, School of Education, St. Cloud State University, St. Cloud, MN, USA
[b]Free Geek, Portland, OR, USA

Abstract

This chapter examines how selected accrediting bodies and academic librarians define collection strength and its relationship to student achievement. Standards adopted by accreditation bodies and library associations, such as the Association of Research Libraries, are reviewed to determine the most common ones which are used to assess library collections. Librarians' efforts to define and demonstrate the adequacy of library resources are also examined in light of increased focus on institutional accountability, and requirements to provide planned and documented evidence of student success. Also reviewed are the challenges faced by academic librarians in a shift as they shift from traditional collection-centered philosophies and practices to those which focus on client-centered collection development such as circulation analysis, citation analysis, interlibrary loans, and student satisfaction surveys to determine collection use and relevance. The findings from a review of standards and existing library literature indicated that student use of library collections depends on faculty perceptions of the library and whether they require students to use library resources and services for their research papers. Through marketing strategies, improvement of student awareness of collections and library services, the chapter concludes that multiple collection-related factors influence the academic success of students, not just the size and importance of library collections per se. The significance of the chapter lies in its identification of halting and difficult adjustments in measuring both collection "adequacy" and student achievements.

Keywords: Collection development; assessment; student learning; citation analysis; collection strength; academic libraries

CONTEXTS FOR ASSESSMENT AND OUTCOME EVALUATION IN LIBRARIANSHIP
ADVANCES IN LIBRARIANSHIP, VOL. 35
© 2012 by Emerald Group Publishing Limited
ISSN: 0065-2830
DOI: 10.1108/S0065-2830(2012)0000035009

I. Introduction

Academic librarians have always claimed that the library is an indispensable tool to ensure students' academic achievement. On its face, this claim is reasonable. As faculty require students to complete research assignments from discipline-specific publications, colleges and universities have historically invested in library collections to guarantee access to those resources. Collection management librarians have sought to protect acquisition budgets in the face of decreased funding, in terms of absolute dollars and relative buying power. The argument that students require adequate resources to achieve academic success has become a matter of organizational survival and professional pride. Accrediting bodies also pressure institutions to provide adequate library resources for programs, or risk losing accreditation.

While collection management librarians have employed different types of collection strength analyses which are persuasive with other librarians, it has been much more challenging to convince faculty, administrators, and accrediting bodies that such measures are directly linked to student academic achievement. Will a stronger collection lead to improved achievement, or will a weakened collection lead to worsening of student achievements? These questions are hard to answer because many factors affect how students make constructive use of library resources. Information literacy instruction, liaison programs, reference services, faculty perceptions of librarians, and the quality of library holdings, all influence actual student use of collections.

This chapter examines how accrediting bodies define collection strength, and how they define and assess the role of academic libraries in providing resources and services which support institutional and curricular goals. It also addresses possible strategies to isolate the impact of library collections on student achievement, and frames measures of collection strength in ways that are compelling to faculty, administrators, and accrediting bodies. Since most of the literature about assessing student achievement has been about undergraduate education, this chapter focuses on collections that support undergraduate curricula. Since higher education has embraced an assessment culture, this chapter argues for assessing collection strength vis-à-vis institutional goals in place of librarian-generated standards.

II. Accreditation and Academic Libraries

A. National Accreditation Infrastructure

For readers not familiar with the system of higher education in the United States, a brief overview is provided here.

The United States Department of Education (USDE) recognizes accrediting agencies that the Secretary of Education "determines to be reliable authorities as to the quality of education or training provided by the institutions of higher education and the higher education programs they accredit" (2012a). According to the USDE Education Database of Accredited Postsecondary Institutions and Programs, "the goal of accreditation is to ensure that education provided by institutions of higher education meets acceptable levels of quality" (p. 1). While USDE does not define quality of library collections, it does define basic accreditation procedures and has authority as follows:

1. Verifying that an institution or program meets established standards;
2. Assisting prospective students in identifying acceptable institutions;
3. Assisting institutions in determining the acceptability of transfer credits;
4. Helping to identify institutions and programs for the investment of public and private funds;
5. Protecting an institution against harmful internal and external pressure;
6. Creating goals for self-improvement of weaker programs and stimulating a general raising of standards among educational institutions;
7. Involving the faculty and staff comprehensively in institutional evaluation and planning;
8. Establishing criteria for professional certification and licensure and for upgrading courses offering such preparation; and
9. Providing one of several considerations used as a basis for determining eligibility for Federal assistance (U.S. Department of Education, 2012b, p. 2).

As of early 2012, USDE had approved 80 national, regional, faith related, career related and program based accrediting organizations. An overarching, voluntary association, the Council for Higher Education Accreditation (CHEA), provides oversight of accrediting agencies and coordinates activities of members in the United States. All college and universities, as institutions, are accredited in their entirety through regional associations. There are currently six, some of which have recognized subdivisions:

1. Middle States Association of Colleges and Schools
   - The Middle States Commission on Higher Education (MSACS-MSCHE);
2. The New England Association of Schools and Colleges
   - Commission on Institutions of Higher Education (NEASC-CIHE);
3. North Central Association of Colleges and Schools
   - The Higher Learning Commission (NCA-HLC);
4. The Northwest Commission on Colleges and Universities (NWCCU);
5. The Southern Association of Colleges and Schools (SACS);
6. The Western Association of Schools and Colleges (WASC).

The standards of the above six regional accreditation agencies along with the Association Council for Independent Colleges and Schools (ACICS), formed the basis of this chapter's review of how library collections have been gauged in terms of adequacy. ACICS is a national organization which accredits professional, technical, and occupational degree granting institutions.

B. Accreditation and Library Collections

Academic library resources and services are usually subject to review by all types of accreditation agencies, be they program specific, regional, or national like ACICS. The definition of "quality" of library resources and services varies, as does the type of information requested by each agency, and the data collection methods employed. While adjectives such as "sufficient" and "adequate" are used to describe library resources and services, these terms are rarely defined. Similarly, the assessment methods are seldom provided. Assessment tools such as student use of print and online resources and their impact on student academic performance, are not always taken into account when evaluating collection strength.

Table 1 summarizes whether or not seven accrediting bodies address five main requirements for academic library collections, according to their standards and guidelines:

1. that the collection should be *appropriate* for the mission and curriculum;
2. the collection should contain *adequate* resources;
3. use of the collection should be taught (*instruction*);
4. the library collection should be *assessed* for relevance on a regular basis;
5. the collection should be *secure*.

Table 1
Inclusion of Main Requirements in Accreditation Standards

	Appropriate collection	Adequate collection	Collection instruction	Collection assessed	Collection secure	Vols. in collection	Library sq. ft.
ACICS	x	x		x			
HLC	x		x	x			
MSCHE	x	x	x				
NEASC	x	x		x			
NWCCU	x	x	x	x	x		
SACS	x	x	x	x			
WASC	x						
Total	7	5	4	5	1	0	0

Sources: Accrediting Council for Independent Colleges and Schools (2011) and Higher Learning Commission (2003).

Also included in the table are two requirements which historically have been valued by institutions—the number of *volumes* held and the *square footage* occupied by libraries.

All seven institutional accrediting bodies believe that library collections should support the institutional mission and curricula "appropriately." Four of the seven require that instruction about library resources and services be given by postsecondary institutions. Five of the seven agencies required that collections be "adequate" and that they be regularly assessed. If teaching faculty use the library resources to support curricula, as NCCU explicitly requires (2E.2), they would learn firsthand whether or not the existing collection meets student needs. NCCU (2E.2) also requires that librarians develop their collections using feedback from users while other agencies imply assessment requirements, that collection strength, user satisfaction, and student academic success are interrelated.

While five of the accrediting bodies explicitly stated that the library should provide "adequate" resources," none provided guidelines for the number of volumes a collection should hold, nor the square footage a library should have—both traditional measures of library adequacy. In fact, several explicitly repudiate these metrics as irrelevant to describing collection strength or library quality. At the same time however, some accrediting bodies still request information about library volume counts, square footage, and expenditures. If the accrediting agencies provide no definitions of adequate library resources, or how to measure this, it seems that institutions are left to devise their own measures, either through user feedback mechanisms or through peer comparison.

While they may not provide specific examples of strong collections or directives about assessing collection strength, accrediting bodies do demand that academic libraries serve students and faculty, and affirm that the value of a library collection is determined by how well it supports the needs of students as well as the institution as a whole. For this reason, assessment of collection strength must take into account the use of library resources by students, as well as their level of satisfaction with resources of all kinds.

C. Library Association and Professional Standards for Collections

Historically, academic libraries—particularly at research institutions—have measured their value by the number of volumes in a collection, as well as the square footage of the library and in some instances, quantitative measures such as materials expenditures, material usage, and reference transactions. Despite attempts to shift to qualitative measures of library adequacy, academic libraries still emphasize these quantitative data which are reflected in annual reports and used as benchmarks for comparison among self-selected peer groups. Likewise, the national organizations which collect data continue to focus, not on outcomes from use of library resources, but rather on quantitative and traditional data.

1. National Center for Education Statistics

The National Center for Education Statistics (NCES), the primary federal entity for collecting and analyzing education data conducts a biennial Academic Library Survey to collect quantitative data about library resources and services during one fiscal year. It reports what is spent on library materials for collections and the number of items in different formats that are acquired and weeded. The survey also asks about the number of items that circulated, the number of library instruction sessions, and reference transactions (National Center for Education Statistics, 2011). NCES does not use the data to determine the "quality" of an academic library or its collections and provide no indicators which link library resources to student success.

2. Association of Research Libraries

The Association of Research Libraries (ARL) collects quantitative data annually from its member libraries. In terms of collections, ARL's reports material expenditures and the number of items in various formats that were acquired and weeded. The reports also include other expenditures, staffing, and service activities of the member libraries (ARL, 2011). Like NCES, ARL does not addresses how library collections and expenditures contribute to student achievement.

3. Association of College and Research Libraries

Only the Association of College & Research Libraries (ACRL) has begun to develop standards for libraries which address the effectiveness and strength of library collections relative to student achievement (ACRL, 2011a). ACRL established their standards "to guide academic libraries in advancing and sustaining their role as partners in educating students, achieving their institutions' missions, and positioning libraries as leaders in assessment and continuous improvement on their campuses" (ACRL, 2011b). The latest version differs from previous versions, articulating the new expectations for library contributions to institutional effectiveness. The standards contain Principles, Performance Indicators, and Sample Outcomes. In Table 2,

Table 2
ACRL Standards Relative to Institutional Accreditation Criteria

	Appropriate collection	Adequate collection	Collection instruction	Collection assessed	Collection secure	Vols. in collection	Library sq. ft.
ACRL	x	x	x	x			

Source: ACRL (2011b).

ACRL's standards for collections are compared with the measures in Table 1 used by institutional accreditation agencies.

During a webinar about the new standards (ACRL, 2011a), the Chair of the ACRL Standards Committee, Patricia Iannuzzi, stated that traditional volume counts are no longer an indicator of quality and depth (2011). At that time, she provided no other information to define quality and depth of an academic library collection. Since ACRL provides no definitions for "quality," "depth," and "diversity," librarians have to devise their own definitions of collection strength, benchmarks, and assessment instruments.

D. Determining Collection Strength in Academic Libraries

1. Defining Collection Strength

In the past academic librarians defined the strength of a collection based on the number of librarian-approved and subject-specific books. Collection holdings were compared against reading lists in various disciplines. If a collection included a majority of the titles, librarians believed that they had built a strong collection. As web-based resources emerged and collections budgets decreased, academic librarians had to begin to reassess collection development strategies as well as definitions of collection strength. A variety of methods emerged which attempted to provide indicators of strength.

Circulation statistics. If the "adequate" and "relevant" terms used by accreditors, were to be defined by frequency of use, then collection strength could be determined through general circulation statistics or the number of "hits" or uses of electronic sites. Each item would have a perceived "value" based on its number of loans and browses. If more than half of the resources had circulated or been visited at least once in recent history, librarians determined which areas of a collection were most "adequate" and "relevant" and would purchase or add resources based on user preferences (Brush, 2007; Littman & Connaway, 2004; Mortimore, 2005; Ochola, 2003).

Citation analysis. In some cases, "collection strength" was defined in whole or in part as the percentage of library resources cited in student research papers (Kille & Henson, 2011; Knight-Davis & Sung, 2008; Leiding, 2005). The higher the percentage of library owned/accessed resources that were used, the more "adequate" the library resources would deemed to be. Such assessments could determine which parts of library collections provided curriculum support and which needed further development. Citation analysis of student and faculty research papers could be used to drive collection development by format as well as subject.

Student satisfaction surveys. Some academic libraries ask users to define collection strength and "adequate resources" through surveys. Collection-related survey questions include use of the library books, journals, and online resources, etc. and whether or not users learned how to search for and access library materials, and whether or not those library resources were helpful for assignments (Inkster, 2010; Weaver, 1999). Students could provide their reasons for satisfaction or dissatisfaction, as well as suggestions for improvement. Such surveys help to determine whether or not accessibility or awareness, in addition to collection quality, influence student satisfaction with the library resources.

Interlibrary loan statistics. If an academic library serves external users "collection strength" might be derived from data analysis of use patterns. Similarly if a high percentage of resources in particular subject areas, are requested frequently through interlibrary loan, those resources might be perceived as "valuable" and be retained (Mortimore, 2005; Ochola, 2003). If institutional goals include service to the community, interlibrary loan statistics and use of accessible online resources could be used to demonstrate the role of libraries in meeting this goal.

Enterprise data management. In the 21st century, some academic librarians have employed data mining to determine which online resources get the most use and who uses them. Such data are used not only to assess use of library collections, but also to "advertise" library resources of interest based on the number of page clicks and page visits. For example, librarians at the University of Minnesota have built a "MyLibrary" portal for web users, based on their relationships to an academic department, degree program, or professional position. The portal tracks usage of online databases and journals through "affinity strings" (Hanson, Nackerud, & Jensen, 2008). Enterprise data management has the potential to increase use of library resources by personalizing recommendations for each individual user, thus providing a new way to perceive and report "adequacy" of library resources.

E. Relationship between Library Instruction and Collection Strength

Awareness of library resources and services will help to drive student use of collections. An accurate assessment of collection strength, regardless of definition, must include recognition and assessment of librarians' efforts to promote resources and services. Shifting from traditional methods to a client-centered collection development philosophy and practice, will require analysis of how faculty integrate library resources into the teaching and learning processes. Evidence from such studies has the potential to show the relationship between collection strength and student success, as well as the role that reference and instruction play in educating users.

Oakleaf summarized this well by asking a critical question:

> Librarians can undertake systematic reviews of course content, readings, reserves, and assignments ... librarians should use this process to track the integration of library resources into the teaching and learning processes of their institution ... What do library services and resources enable students to do or do better? (2011, pp. 95–96)

In short, librarians and others need to know what has changed or improved in terms of students' skills, attitudes, knowledge, behaviors, status, or life conditions as a result of their use of library collections. In order to know that these changes or improvements are in line with institutional goals for student learning outcomes, librarians need reliable information about what those outcomes are and what success looks like.

1. Documenting Student Learning

According to all the accreditation and library standards discussed above, academic libraries must support the goals of their parent institutions. All of the accreditation organizations discussed in this chapter identify "support and promotion of student learning," in one incantation or another, as a major institutional goal, under which all others fall. Yet "student learning" is a broader, more elusive concept than is "academic achievement."

The Higher Learning Commission (HLC) does not provide a definition of student learning in any of its documents. Instead, it presents six "fundamental questions" to institutions:

1. How are your stated student learning outcomes appropriate to your mission, programs, degrees, and students?
2. What evidence do you have that students achieve your stated learning outcomes?

3. In what ways do you analyze and use evidence of student learning?
4. How do you ensure shared responsibility for student learning and for assessment of student learning?
5. How do you evaluate and improve the effectiveness of your efforts to assess and improve student learning?
6. In what ways do you inform the public and other stakeholders about what students are learning—and how well? (2007, p. 1)

While institutions can prove that students passed courses and earned degrees, it is more difficult to prove that students actually learned and retained information, that they were affected by the information, and—even more difficult to prove—that they used library resources and services to do so. Surveys or interviews with students about their learning experiences, use of the library, and how the library improved or enhanced learning experiences, may be more valid measures of how well the institution met its primary goal.

2. Faculty Perceptions and Involvement

Faculty perceptions about library resources and services affect how and if students are directed to use library collections for their work. According to Schonfeld and Housewright (2010), over time faculty have become less likely to perceive libraries as the "gateway" to information, and more likely to perceive them as the "buyer." The perception of library as "buyer" often affects perception of librarians as fellow educators, even though some library and information science programs prepare librarians to teach (Wyss, 2010). At the same time, faculty members believe that students must learn information literacy, traditionally the realm of librarians (DaCosta, 2010; Gullikson, 2006). An exception to this rule are faculty who teach distance and online courses, in which case more than half provide all of the research materials needed by their students, and do not require use of a library (Cahoy & Moyo, 2007).

3. Information Literacy and Instruction

While faculty members often teach students how to evaluate and analyze resources in discipline-specific contexts, librarians usually focus on locating resources in the online catalog and library databases, differentiating between popular and scholarly journal articles, and citations (DaCosta, 2010; Gullikson, 2006). This would imply that students who receive library instruction would gain awareness of library resources, actively use them for research assignments, and record their use in bibliographies (DaCosta, 2010).

Student bibliographies often indicate faculty and librarian involvement in their research process and, according to DaCosta (2010) faculty who do not include library instruction as part of their coursework receive student papers of lower "academic quality."

Focus on information literacy can however lead to an imbalanced view of outcomes assessment in libraries. ACRL's (2011b) latest standards provided examples of outcomes as follows:

1. Faculty and students can access collections needed for educational and research needs from all user locations.
2. Users demonstrate effective access to library resources no matter what their starting point.
3. Users expand the types of sources (e.g., multiple formats—books, journals, primary sources, etc.) consulted when doing research as a result of a one-on-one consultation with librarians.
4. Users readily transfer the skills learned through one-on-one consultation with a librarian to other research contexts/assignments.
5. Students discover the appropriate library resources needed for their coursework.
6. Users characterize the library interface as easy to find and intuitive to navigate.
7. Users judge the library as up-to-date in methods provided for access.
8. Users judge integration of library interfaces and resources found through the library as one reason for their success.
9. Faculty and students judge access to collections sufficient to support their educational and research needs.
10. Faculty, students, and community users are satisfied with the collections provided by libraries for their educational, business, and research needs.

Measuring and validating such outcomes remains unclear to many. What are the indicators (i.e., what percent and number users "discover ... appropriate library resources ... ")? What should be the data sources, at what intervals should these data be collected, and most importantly, how can immediate, intermediate, and long-term outcomes be measured with respect to use of library collections? The choice of data sources for such assessments can include pre and posttest, observation, professional assessments, academic records, portfolios, surveys, and focus groups to name a few. Institutional or library-based assessments require knowledge of such tools and the capacity to execute them—both of which may be in short supply.

At the same time neither definitions nor validated measurement tools exist to determine collection strengths. Client-centered collection development, however, has clearly become a best practice in academic libraries that serve undergraduates. Unfortunately, collection strength is rarely linked with student achievement in the literature. Three recent studies point to potential methods show results that could potentially link student achievement with collection strength.

Leiding (2005) applied citation analysis to a sample of the bibliographies of undergraduate honors theses submitted by students for mandatory portfolios from 1993 to 2002. A stratified sample of 101 theses was selected with a total number of 3564 citations of which 3407 were unique. Of the total, 1238 or 36.3% were books, 1410 or 41.4% were journals, and the remaining 759 were other types of materials such as newspapers, primary sources, web sites (beginning 1997), and government documents. Table 3 shows the extent to which the institution's library had the materials used in its collections.

The study found an increase in journal citations over time, presumably due to increased access to online resources and the increased percentage of acquisitions budgets devoted to serials and databases. Findings did not support the hypothesis that the use of web citations would increase, partially due to faculty advisement and the fact that the early iterations of the web were not viewed as sources of scholarly material. Leiding's study provided a baseline to track trends in use of online sources and journals, and it pointed to a methodology that can be used "to evaluate how well collections are responding to changing research demands (Leiding, p. 428).

Citation analysis was also used by Knight-Davis and Sung (2008) on undergraduate papers submitted as part of writing portfolios throughout their programs from 2000 to 2005. The study was done to provide baseline data for future information literacy programs and to collect evidence that could guide collection development. A random sample of 957 papers from 312 portfolios of which 293 had no citations or reference lists which resulted in 420 papers with a total of 1961 citations for analysis.

Analysis of the data showed that of all types of materials, 587 (30.5%) were from books, 559 (28.5%) were from web sites, and 534 (27.2%) were from journals. The study also revealed "papers with more citations will

Table 3
Number and Percent of Cited Materials Available Locally

Books (N)	1,238
Books (%)	65.4
Journals (N)	1,410
Journals (%)	58.2
Other (N)	538
Other (%)	48.9

typically have a higher word count" (p. 450) which could mean more detailed and thoughtful arguments, and thus higher achievement levels. In terms of comparison with Leiding, Table 4 provides data indicating the percentages of library holdings reflected in the cited works. Of the total citations, 559 or 57% were to online sources of all types including e-books, ejournals, and databases.

The authors concluded that the study did provide insights which would be used to improve library instruction programs. They also concluded that the sources used by students are often "heavily influenced by [faculty] requirements … in the paper assignment" (p. 457).

Kille and Henson (2011) conducted a small pilot citation analysis in 2010–2011 of undergraduate papers by students in the Environmental Studies program at Naropa University. The papers had been included in the university's 2009 assessment portfolio for an accreditation self-study report. The authors used a coverage power test of collection strength (White, 2008) for specific academic disciplines. The study addressed two narrowly focused research questions which were:

- Is there a correlation between disciplinary collection strength and achievement of student learning outcomes across departments?
- Is there a correlation between library collections usage and achievement of student learning outcomes within a given department?

The results showed no correlation between student academic achievement and either the number of citations or the percent of locally owned resources. Nothing interesting or significant emerged in the analysis of statistical relationships. The range of coverage power scores was fairly small, while the range of assessment scores was fairly broad. One possible interpretation of these results is that students with better-assessed papers made the best

Table 4
Number of Percent of Cited Materials Held by the Library

Books (N)	587
Books (%)	69.2
Journals (N)	534
Journals (%)	80.0
Other (N)[a]	840
Other (%)	N/A

[a]"Other" included online resources.

possible use of available resources even if they were weak, while students with worse-assessed papers made poor use of available resources, however strong those resources might have been.

The papers which cited a large percentage of resources not held by the Naropa University Library received excellent assessment score, as did papers receiving worse assessment scores. At the same time, papers citing a large percentage of locally held resources received excellent assessment scores, as did papers receiving worse assessment scores. One possible interpretation is that having students making good use of available resources is more important than the adequacy and appropriateness of the available resources. It is difficult to draw useful conclusions from a comparison of the results of these three studies. Leiding (2005) de-duplicated citations, that is, if 40 different students each cited *The Grapes of Wrath* once in assignments, and 1 student cited *The Return of the King* once, both instances were counted as one cited book. This de-duplication made the results difficult to use in comparison to similar studies. The percentage of locally owned materials cited is an important measure because it speaks directly to how students engage with collections. Therefore, it makes a difference if, say, 90% of books cited are locally owned even if only 65% of them are unique titles in the collection.

III. Research Challenges and Limitations

The challenges and limitations of doing research into relationships between collection strength and student achievement fall into three broad categories: theoretical, practical, and cultural. Theoretical challenges and limitations involve conflict or confusion about conceptual frameworks, the definitions of terms, and the methods of gathering and interpreting data. Practical ones involve technological, legal, financial, and other structural barriers to a particular line of research. Cultural challenges and limitations involve problems that may have theoretical and practical solutions but which are unacceptable to a community.

A. Theoretical Challenges

One major theoretical challenge is choosing what to measure. Collection evaluation based on holdings alone tells us nothing about usage, while collection evaluation based on usage alone indicates nothing about effectiveness. Measuring the number of citations in student papers provides information about usage of some (though not all) locally owned materials. Results can potentially address effectiveness when paired with evaluation of the quality of student papers. Another theoretical issue is identification of trends in student research habits and advances in library technology. Defining the significance of local ownership and the meaning of local ownership in an environment of hosted content and services add more questions to be addressed.

In the past librarians understood collections to be assets: resources which are acquired and held. In today's changing libraries, collections are better understood as services. An Ithaka survey notes a "significant shift in expenditures away from monographs and towards journals over the past decades," with journals expenditures in libraries now averaging 88% digital and 12% print (Long & Schonfeld, p. 28). Publishers, including Oxford University Press and Cambridge University Press, have also introduced subscription models for e-books alongside purchasing options. As a result, libraries are quickly moving into an environment where collection strength cannot be measured without measuring the effectiveness of student-centered library services.

Reference and instruction therefore become critical aspects of what traditionally have been considered collection development issues. If librarians build impressive collections, students will not automatically come and use them. If students do not know how to use the library, or care not to use the library (because faculty have no expectation for the students to do so), then librarians cannot know if collections are strong except by using client-centered methods of collection analysis.

B. Practical Challenges

In their pilot study, Kille and Henson (2011) encountered a number of practical challenges. Only one of three responding departments had usable data, one stated that it had no data, and one had only aggregate student learning outcome data. Thus Kille and Henson could not compare the use of resources across departments. They did establish collection strength scores for individual courses within the one department with usable data. Another limitation was that the data set was very small, with a small number of student assignments had been selected from various courses and assessed by departmental faculty. Further, it was impossible to correlate collection strength with student achievement because the assessment scores were not a continuous scale. Unfortunately, academic departments did not consult with the library about the size of assessment data sets or the assessment methodologies used. A diversity of assessment methodologies across institutions also makes it a challenge to replicate the research. Finally, many library policies and systems enable the capture of data about usage only at a very coarse-grained aggregate level.

C. Cultural Challenges

One cultural challenge is that librarians have traditionally considered evaluation of library materials to be their unique professional domain. Linking collection strength to student achievement cedes some of that territory to administrators and accrediting bodies (Wolff, 1995). At the same time, teaching faculty are feeling a shift in the balance of shared governance in favor of administrators (Tuchman, 2009). Outcome assessment by academic libraries is becoming the last, best hope and the tool to obtain financial, political, and internal moral support. In the corporately influenced field of higher education, everything comes down to the bottom line of reputation or revenue or both, as it operates more and more under what Tuchman (2009) calls an accountability regime.

Surviving and thriving in an accountability regime will require that libraries consider the ways external stakeholders may react to results which may not show a clear connection between library collections and improved student learning outcomes (Dugan & Hernon, 2002). Since librarians cannot assess collection strength with reference to universal standards, they must carefully design their assessment efforts to ensure that reports to stakeholders can highlight the positive work done by librarians and teaching faculty and show where the library may need more financial support from the administration.

According to accreditation and library association standards, academic libraries must support the goals of their institutions. The accreditation organizations documents studied by the authors also identified "support and promotion of student learning" as a major institutional goal, under which all others fall. "Student learning" is a broader, more elusive concept than "academic achievement." Yet both lack solid definitions, which again gives library outcomes assessment external cultural constraints.

IV. Conclusions and Recommendations for Future Research

If library collections are indeed assessed, a review of the literature should show studies of outcomes linked to library collections that are appropriate, adequate, and the subject of instruction for students. The literature, however, largely focuses on assessment of outcomes linked to instruction. The three studies reported in this chapter did not provide conclusive results and provided only partial models for future research.

Whether prior research used quantitative or qualitative methods, more research is clearly needed before conclusions can be drawn about the relationship between collection strength and student achievement. This future research will need to take into account the theoretical, practical, and cultural challenges that have made conclusive results difficult to achieve thus far.

Numerous opportunities exist for interesting and meaningful research into the relationship between collection strength and ACRL's 10 sample outcomes. For example, researchers could study whether students can access collections from on-campus and distance locations by pairing citation analysis and assessment of assignments in courses that have online and classroom sections to determine if the quality of assignments differ between on-campus and distance students. Researchers could also determine whether students increase their usage of different types of information resources after one-on-one consultation with a librarian, or whether library instruction is effective with observable and measurable outcomes. The only limit on these kinds of research projects—other than the perennial questions of time and money—is the creativity and persistence of researchers.

Time and money are very real limits to thorough assessment, but an increasing urgency to defend staff and resources must push librarians to share measurable outcomes of library effectiveness with external stakeholders. These following recommendations for future research will enable librarians to develop the assessment tools that they need:

1. Prioritize access over ownership when studying library collections that support undergraduate education.
2. Focus on producing significant results, in particular with large data sets.
3. Provide methodologies and results which are replicable.
4. Lay the groundwork for more finely grained future analyses.
5. Ensure that research is collaborative.
6. Report not only what their results say, but what they mean.

One potentially productive research program might begin with an extremely brief qualitative survey of undergraduate students that attempts to provide researchers with answers to the following questions:

1. Are library interfaces easy to find and intuitive to navigate?
2. Are accessible collections sufficient to support their educational and research needs?
3. Are library interfaces and resources as one reason for their success?

4. What is the respondent's current or anticipated major?
5. Is the respondent willing to participate in a more detailed survey?

In short, the profession has more opportunities to explore than it has answers at this stage.

References

Accrediting Council for Independent Colleges and Schools. (2011). *Accreditation criteria—Policies, procedures, and standards: 3-1-800: Library resources and services*. Retrieved from http://www.acics.org/publications/criteria.aspx#3-1-800

Association of College & Research Libraries. (2011a). *ACRL standards webcast recording*. Retrieved from http://learningtimesevents.org/acrl/acrl-stds-archive/

Association of College & Research Libraries. (2011b). *Standards for libraries in higher education*. Retrieved from http://www.ala.org/ala/mgrps/divs/acrl/standards/standardslibraries.cfm

Association of Research Libraries. (2011). *ARL statistics*. Retrieved from http://www.arl.org/stats/annualsurveys/arlstats/index.shtml

Brush, D. (2007). Circulation analysis of an engineering monograph approval plan. *Collection Building, 26*(2), 59–62.

Cahoy, E. S., & Moyo, L. M. (2007). Faculty perspectives on e-learners' library research needs. *Journal of Library & Information Services in Distance Learning, 2*(4), 1–17.

DaCosta, J. W. (2010). Is there an information literacy skills gap to be bridged? An examination of faculty perceptions and activities relating to information literacy in the United States and England. *College & Research Libraries, 71*(3), 203–222.

Dugan, R. E., & Hernon, P. (2002). Outcomes assessment: Not synonymous with inputs and outputs. *The Journal of Academic Librarianship, 28*(6), 376–380.

Gullikson, S. (2006). Faculty perceptions of ACRL's information literacy standards for higher education. *Journal of Academic Librarianship, 32*(6), 583–592.

Hanson, C., Nackerud, S., & Jensen, K. (2008, December 15). Affinity strings: Enterprise data management for resource recommendations. *Code4Lib*, (5). Retrieved from http://journal.code4lib.org/articles/501

Higher Learning Commission. (2003). *Handbook of accreditation*. Chicago, IL: Author. Retrieved from http://www.ncahlc.org/Information-for-Institutions/publications.html

Higher Learning Commission. (2007). *Student learning, assessment, and accreditation*. Retrieved from http://www.ncahlc.org/Information-for-Institutions/publications.html

Iannuzzi, P. (2011). ACRL standards for libraries in higher education 2011. *Presentations (Libraries)*, Paper 73. Retrieved from http://digitalcommons.library.unlv.edu/libfactpresentation/73

Inkster, C. (2010). *Miller Center student survey {Paper survey instrument}*. St. Cloud, MN: Saint Cloud State University.

Kille, M., & Henson, A. (2011, May). Using academic course data to assess library collection strength. Paper present at the Acquisitions Institute at Timberline,

Timberline Lodge, OR. Retrieved from http://www.acquisitionsinstitute.org/2011acquisitionsinstitute

Knight-Davis, S., & Sung, J. S. (2008). Analysis of citations in undergraduate papers. *College & Research Libraries, 69*(5), 447–458.

Leiding, R. (2005). Using citation checking of undergraduate honors thesis bibliographies to evaluate library collections. *College & Research Libraries, 66*(5), 417–429.

Littman, J., & Connaway, L. S. (2004). A circulation analysis of print books and e-books in an academic research library. *Library Resources & Technical Services, 48*(4), 256–262.

Long, M., & Schonfeld, R. (2010). *Ithaka S+R survey 2010: Insights from U.S. academic library directors.* Retrieved from http://www.ithaka.org/ithaka-s-r/research/ithaka-s-r-library-survey-2010

Middle States Commission on Higher Education. (2006). *Characteristics of excellence in higher education: Requirements of affiliation and standards for accreditation.* Philadelphia, PA: Author. Retrieved from http://www.msche.org/publications/CHX-2011-WEB.pdf

Mortimore, J. M. (2005). Access-informed collection development and the academic library: Using holdings, circulation data, and ILL to develop prescient collections. *Collection Management, 30*(3), 21–37.

National Center for Education Statistics. (2011). *Library statistics program.* Retrieved from http://nces.ed.gov/surveys/libraries/

National Center for Education Statistics. (n.d.). *Academic library survey.* Retrieved from http://nces.ed.gov/%20homepage

New England Association of Schools and Colleges. (2011). *Standards for accreditation: Standard seven: Library and other information resources.* Bedford, MA: Author. Retrieved from http://cihe.neasc.org/standards_policies/standards/standards_html_version#standard_seven

Northwest Commission on Colleges and Universities. (2010). *Standards for accreditation.* Retrieved from http://www.nwccu.org/Pubs%20Forms%20and%20Updates/Publications/Standards%20for%20Accreditation.pdf

Oakleaf, M. (2011). Are they learning? Are we? Learning outcomes and the academic library. *Library Quarterly, 81*(1), 61–82.

Ochola, J. N. (2003). Use of circulation statistics and interlibrary loan data in collection management. *Collection Management, 27*(1), 1–13.

Schonfeld, R. C., & Housewright, R. (2010). *Ithaka S+R faculty survey 2009: Key strategic insights for libraries, publishers, and societies.* New York, NY: Ithaka S+R. Retrieved from http://www.ithaka.org/ithaka-s-r/research/faculty-surveys-2000-2009/Faculty%20Study%202009.pdf

Southern Association of Colleges and Schools Commission on Colleges. (2010). *The principles of accreditation: Foundations for quality enhancement.* Decatur, GA: Author. Retrieved from http://www.sacscoc.org/pdf/2010principlesofacreditation.pdf

Tuchman, G. (2009). *Wannabe U: Inside the corporate university.* Chicago, IL: University of Chicago Press.

United States Department of Education. (2012a). *College accreditation in the United States* (p. 1). Retrieved from http://www2.ed.gov/admins/finaid/accred/accreditation.html#Overview

United States Department of Education. (2012b). *College accreditation in the United States* (p. 2). Retrieved from http://www2.ed.gov/admins/finaid/accred/accreditation_pg2.html

Weaver, P. (1999). A student centered classroom-based approach to collection building. *The Journal of Academic Librarianship*, 25(3), 202–210.

Western Association of Schools and Colleges Accrediting Commission for Senior Colleges and Universities. (2008). *Handbook of accreditation*. Burlingame, CA: Author. Retrieved from http://www.wascsenior.org/findit/files/forms/Handbook_of_Accreditation.pdf

White, H. D. (2008). Better than brief tests: Coverage power tests of collection strength. *College & Research Libraries*, 69(2), 155–174.

Wolff, R. A. (1995). Using the accreditation process to transform the mission of the library. *New Directions for Higher Education*, 90, 77–91. doi:10.1002/he.369959008.

Wyss, P. A. (2010). Library school faculty member perceptions regarding faculty status for academic librarians. *College & Research Libraries*, 71(4), 375–388.

Online Educational Case Studies

Learning Outcomes Assessment via Electronic Portfolios

Rachel Applegate and Marilyn M. Irwin

School of Library and Information Science, Indiana University, Indianapolis, IN, USA

Abstract

Accreditation agencies both institutional and professional (such as the American Library Association) have asked educators to demonstrate student learning outcomes for every academic program that they are assessing, and that they use the data gathered for continuous improvement of programs. This chapter reports on the development of an electronic portfolio (ePortfolio) structure for accomplishing an assessment process within a school of library and information science. From the student side, the portfolio prompts them to select work that they feel is their best effort for each program outcome such as "assist and educate users." From the faculty side, all items for a given outcome can be downloaded and assessed quantitatively and qualitatively so as to arrive at an understanding of how well the program as a whole is doing, with sufficient detail to guide specific improvement decisions. During design, researchers employed a sequential qualitative feedback system to pose tasks (usability testing) and gather commentaries (through interviews) from students while faculty debated the efficacy of this approach and its place within the school's curricular structure. The local end product was a usable portfolio system implemented within a course management system (Oncourse/Sakai). The generalizable outcome is an understanding of key elements necessary for ePortfolios to function as a program-level assessment system: a place for students to select and store artifacts, a way for faculty to access and review the artifacts, simple aggregations of scoring and qualitative information, and a feedback loop of results into program design for improved student learning.

Keywords: Program evaluation; accreditation; electronic portfolios; student learning outcomes assessment; LIS education

I. Introduction

One of the most significant movements in higher education over the past 20 years has been an increased emphasis on accountability in terms of assessment and outcomes measurement. No longer could institutions base reporting and

CONTEXTS FOR ASSESSMENT AND OUTCOME EVALUATION IN LIBRARIANSHIP
ADVANCES IN LIBRARIANSHIP, VOL. 35
© 2012 by Emerald Group Publishing Limited
ISSN: 0065-2830
DOI: 10.1108/S0065-2830(2012)0000035010

rankings on quantities of inputs or resources, such as student-faculty ratios, percent of faculty possessing the Ph.D., grade point averages of applicants, or numbers of enrollees. Instead, federal, state legislative, and popular (consumer) sentiment turned towards asking what colleges and universities were accomplishing with and for their students: namely outcomes, not outputs. The US Department of Education, which recognizes accrediting agencies, began requiring that the institutions and programs they review document the evaluation of student learning outcomes with assessment in order to have a record of data-driven improvements. This was based on longstanding guidelines (from 1965), and formalized in amendments to US federal law that were passed in 2008.

Assessment itself has always been a vital part of academia in two important ways: individual accomplishment on specific tasks (papers, projects, tests: assignments and course grades) and the success of graduates (employment and subsequent accomplishments). These were individually oriented assessments, with little explicit linkage between the two. Professors assessed in-course performance, and program chairs (and marketers) cared about how their graduates fared.

A new component in assessment focused on something broader than the individual student, and was more closely tied to how a program worked, namely how a *program* is doing overall, in terms of students' accomplishing specified outcomes. For example, individual students may pass or fail a general exam. If many fail, there is a program-level problem. It may be an incorrect exam that does not measure what the program aims to produce (deficient measurement), or it could be poor preparation of students (deficient education). In an assessment feedback loop, either the measure would be changed, or faculty would look to see where they are not covering, or emphasizing, or integrating, the desired knowledge, skills, or competencies.

II. Library and Information Science Education Assessment

For schools of library and information science (LIS), in the United States, Canada, and Puerto Rico, accredited to offer masters degrees by the American Library Association (ALA), the assessment component is expressed in the Standards for Accreditation as follows:

I. Mission: (subsection 3)
Within the context of these Standards each program is judged on the degree to which it attains its objectives. In accord with the mission of the school, clearly defined, publicly stated, and regularly reviewed program goals and objectives form the essential frame of

reference for meaningful external and internal evaluation. The evaluation of program goals and objectives involves those served: students, faculty, employers, alumni, and other constituents.

II. Curriculum: (subsection 7)

The curriculum is continually reviewed and receptive to innovation; its evaluation is used for ongoing appraisal, to make improvements, and to plan for the future. Evaluation of the curriculum includes assessment of students' achievements and their subsequent accomplishments.

VI: Students: (subsection 6)

The school applies the results of evaluation of student achievement to program development. Procedures are established for systematic evaluation of the degree to which a program's academic and administrative policies and activities regarding students are accomplishing its objectives.

(American Library Association, 2008)

Within ALA's framework of MLS program content (e.g., organization of information, research competence, user education) each program determines its own mission and student learning goals, decides how to measure attainment, and documents what it does with the results. Outcomes for students in a particular program will combine the essence of librarianship with the mission of that particular institution. Measurement needs to be valid, reliable, and feasible. That is, the methods of measuring need to be true to the desired outcomes, provide consistent information, and not overburden those who participate.

Program-level assessment of student learning means aggregating data from direct and indirect measures of student learning. In the early 2000s, LIS programs primarily employed indirect measures as a measure of program assessment (Applegate, 2006). Indirect measures included such things as exit surveys or interviews, placement rates, student evaluations of teaching, and cumulative GPAs (see Palomba & Banta, 1999).

Measures are "direct" when they provide specific, detailed, and valid measurements of student knowledge and skills. These methods such as tests, projects, and observed demonstrations are very common within courses as the means to assess individuals (Suskie, 2009). Other direct measures can be added at the program level, such as national standardized exams, local comprehensive exams, capstone projects, or summative presentations.

A. Portfolio Assessment

A portfolio consists of an individual's collection of artifacts—projects, papers, observer evaluations, personal reflections, etc. While some portfolio designs include student reflections on their learning (which are indirect measures as far as examining actual skills or knowledge) the idea of a portfolio is fundamentally oriented toward *direct* measurement. In addition, a portfolio lifts individual papers, projects, and internship supervisor observations out of the context of individual courses. Each student's portfolio can not only include materials generated for courses but also for extracurricular activities, internship placements, or other program requirements such as comprehensive exams. The sum of all these items can represent the program as a whole in a way that the contents and measurement of an individual course cannot.

In addition, creating a portfolio as such—particularly one oriented around *program goals* rather than a checklist of courses—is a process that itself shows each student how to see the program as a whole instead of as an accumulation of graded credit hours. This is a powerful consideration in library science programs. Most programs provide great flexibility to students, due to the diversity of student backgrounds and the many career paths available in the field, but yet the aim is to have "*coherent* [emphasis added] programs of study" as stated in ALA's standards (IV.4).

Portfolios have been widely adopted for a variety of purposes by educators over the past twenty or so years. There are three main ways to use portfolios, although these are not mutually exclusive categories and each has important subcategories. The main ways are for development, assessment, and showcasing.

1. Development Portfolios

The developmental or learning type of portfolio is one of the most widely used, or at least researched and reported on, types. In a developmental portfolio, for each outcome, students preserve and reflect upon beginning, intermediate, and mastery-level assignments or accomplishments. This process of reflection is consistent with a "constructivist" theory of learning in which this intense form of participation reinforces and deepens student learning. These types of portfolios can be built into individual courses or designed to follow a set of skills, such as writing portfolios (see, e.g., Chitpin & Simon, 2009; Scott, 2005; Shepherd & Hannafin, 2009). While engaging in this developmental reflection has educational benefits, it is also time-consuming on the part of advisors or instructors, and because of that workload, is commonly associated with credit-bearing courses or requirements.

2. Assessment Portfolios

Assessment of individuals and their professional competency based upon how they present themselves and their work in portfolios has a long history. Higher education professors are expected to document their teaching, research, and service activities in dossiers or portfolios (Billings & Kowalski, 2008). This is a balance between areas of competency expected of all tenure-track faculty, on the one hand, and a tremendous variety in how that competency can be manifested in different academic disciplines, on the other hand.

Outside of academia, some established uses are in creative fields such as art and architecture. More recently, it has been massively adopted particularly in education both by schools of education and by state teacher licensing agencies. It is also being used or explored as an alternative in a wide variety of other areas: advanced practice nursing (Byrne, Schroeter, Carter, & Mower, 2009; Taylor, Stewart, & Bidewell, 2009), credit for prior learning (Klein-Collins & Hain, 2009), and music education (Kramer, 2007).

3. Showcase Portfolios

Showcase portfolios allow individuals to present themselves to potential employers using current and job-related media. For people in creative or technology fields, the line between a portfolio that shows proficiency to meet graduation standards and one that displays their competence to employers is essentially erased (Tubaishat, Lansari, & Al-Rawi, 2009).

Using a portfolio in LIS programs is not new, but it has primarily been concerned with assessing students individually with developmental portfolios in specific courses, or graduation-requirement portfolios. At many US institutions, it has only applied to students preparing for licensure as school librarians. It has also only recently been developed in an electronic format as opposed to the giant three-ring binder format. Thus, using an electronic portfolio (*ePortfolio*) structure for *program*-level assessment is a relatively new concept. There are at present only a scattering of reports on the use of this data for program, not student, assessment (Fitch, Reed, Peet, & Tolman, 2008; Gorlewski, 2010; Mercer, 2008;). This study reports on the design of such a system at one ALA-accredited Masters of Library Science program—at Indiana University (IU).

III. Development of an ePortfolio

IU's ePortfolio project was developed as a pilot study at the Indianapolis campus of the School of Library and Information Science (SLIS). IU-SLIS is a school located on two campuses, Bloomington and Indianapolis, with a shared accreditation by the ALA. The school's dean resides on the Bloomington campus, and there are two associate deans, one on each campus. The Bloomington campus offers the Master of Library Science (MLS), Master of Information Science (MIS), Specialist, and Ph.D. degrees; Indianapolis offers the MLS. Admission requirements, curriculum, mission, goals, and objectives are same on both campuses.

The Indianapolis campus schedules course times to fit students who work (evenings, Fridays), and offers web-based courses and courses delivered to several sites around the state by teleconferencing. Its student body is on average older, working, and reliant upon technology for coursework and administrative tasks. IU uses Oncourse, a self-developed course management system with robust storage, data, communication, and custom-design features. The University's information technology (IT) personnel developed an ePortfolio system and provide grants and staff assistance to faculty who use various Oncourse features to improve student learning.

The program goals for the IU-SLIS Master of Library Science are to:

- Assist and educate users of libraries and information centers;
- Develop and manage library collections;
- Organize and represent information resources;
- Apply management and leadership skills;
- Conduct and analyze research;
- Demonstrate basic technical expertise; and
- Approach professional issues with understanding.

The SLIS faculty had determined that there was a need to improve the method used to assess student learning outcomes to meet accreditation requirements which had been revised since the previous accreditation visit. Members of the faculty on the Indianapolis campus developed an ePortfolio for program assessment and improvement for a number of reasons. The benefits of the system are technology integration, program reflection, and the lack of an acceptable alternative.

One decision factor was to compare a portfolio system to other direct measure alternatives. If a capstone were to be introduced, it would lengthen the current 36 credit requirement or displace required courses or electives. If thesis requirements were instituted, it would again lengthen the program for students and also add significantly to faculty workload. Similarly, comprehensive exams would not lengthen the program for students, but would require careful design, impose significant workload on faculty, and require additional labor to aggregate results (as would theses).

A. Benefits

Technology was a prime benefit for process, learning, and administration. Some studies of the implementation of ePortfolios, particularly in teacher education program, reported that many students needed multiple workshops and extensive individual coaching to manage the technological platform (Hyndman, Gray, Pierce, & Hyndman, 2007). This turns into a distinct advantage for LIS program evaluation. Librarianship is an inherently technology-connected profession. It is not only desirable but also essential that graduating students have skills sufficient to master (at least) an ePortfolio system. In that sense, the ability to construct a portfolio itself is a base-line measure of one professional competency.

There were also important administrative benefits. Both faculty and students in this situation (as in many library schools) are often widely scattered geographically. This securely authenticated but web-mounted platform allows for access, administration, and communication from anywhere. While the IU system includes a series of tools for scoring, commenting on, and aggregating evaluative information, any ePortfolio system that includes private, public, and shared areas for storage of artifacts (a cloud configuration) can serve the basic needs of portfolio use.

Finally, this specific system, because it was primarily designed for undergraduate, developmental use, includes a reflection component into its design. Besides the simple storage of specific artifacts, having students provide (brief) reflections added to the evaluators' understanding of those artifacts. More, it turned out to provide beneficial encouragement for students, as they graduated, to have a better understanding of what their degrees—their accumulation of credits, requirements, and electives—added up to.

B. Pilot Study

As the faculty began to explore this option, they received a competitive grant from the Center for Teaching and Learning on the Indianapolis campus to assist in the design phase. A pilot study was undertaken to test the concept and perfect its design in five phases.

- Summer 2009: Students tested basic navigation and understanding of the process;
- Fall 2009: Beginning and graduating students tested navigation and usage with small-scale implementation;
- Spring 2010: Graduating students tested construction of complete portfolios;
- Summer 2010: Faculty members tested navigation, usage, and evaluation of artifacts submitted by the graduating students;
- Fall 2010: Faculty members discussed the outcomes of the pilot and use of the assessment results.

1. Student Testing

Given the experience reported in the literature on portfolios—that students were often challenged by both technology and the conceptual framework of portfolios—a careful and thorough approach was taken to get information from students at various stages of their programs. During the first phases in summer 2009, some design features (or flaws) were noted and reported to the University's IT personnel who made some changes. Not all suggestions were adopted if the needs of one particular user group did not outweigh the priorities of the majority of users, which in the IU system as a whole would be undergraduates.

Phase one. In summer 2009, an ePortfolio site for the MLS was designed. Student users of the site were presented with a matrix listing each of the desired learning outcomes in a column on the left, with corresponding space (cell) in a column on the right in which to load artifacts. Students selected items from any part of their coursework that they felt demonstrated mastery of that outcome. During the pilot, different prompts were tested to see what would be most helpful to users, but would also decrease administrative burdens, with fewer questions and less staff or faculty time.

An option existed within the IU ePortfolio for administrators and faculty to designate particular assignments for automatic submission from all students. This was a feature used in undergraduate implementation, and undoubtedly simplified their portfolio construction. In the MLS ePortfolio, students themselves chose any assignments, from any course. This had several benefits. Students were more personally conscious of the link between assignment and program goal. They had great flexibility in the choice of project from a required class or a more advanced elective. For example, people intending to be public services librarians would have more basic items for the "organization and representation of knowledge" (cataloging) component than for "assist and educate users." In addition, the program's two objectives relating to technology and professional issues were not tied to a specific course in the program. Instead, these could be, and should be, evident in a variety of courses, and students could reflect on their meaning within the context of areas of professional practice.

Participants in the summer of 2009 were students taking a course on evaluation of library sources and services. They represented a variety of interests (public, school, academic) and backgrounds (from paraprofessionals to new college graduates to career changers), because the course is one of two options for a program requirement. They were asked to navigate around the interface, read and reflect on the prompts, consider what items they might select, and give their perspectives on the use of portfolios in program evaluation. At this point, students provided feedback on navigability issues and the kinds of information and instruction that were needed. Site design information was passed on to the University's IT personnel for implementation. Suggestions about instructions were incorporated by SLIS staff into an improved matrix for further testing.

Phase two. In the fall of 2009, there were three groups of participants: students taking an evaluation course, paid volunteers who were beginning the program, and paid volunteers who were close to graduation. The beginners were specifically included based on comments from the summer such as, "I know what this means but I would find it confusing at the beginning." In full implementation, students would ideally be working with their matrix throughout the program, filling in each area as they felt they achieved their best work in it.

IU's Institutional Review Board approved the study design. Volunteers were given a modest stipend to compensate them for their time. For students in the evaluation course, an assignment to critique instructional evaluation was required, but it could be fulfilled either by reviewing the SLIS ePortfolio or in one of two other ways. Most students chose the ePortfolio-review option.

Beginning (first semester) and end (last semester) of program was one demographic division. Another grouping was the type of library the participants were interested in. Participants from the evaluation course included three students with academic library career goals, ten aimed at public libraries, and seven at school libraries. The recruited volunteers consisted of 13 academic library, 3 public library, and 3 school library. Participants navigated around the portfolio and also completed at least one matrix area. They either provided written comments or were interviewed by project staff with comments transcribed by project staff. Contrary to expectations, the students at the beginning of their program did not experience significant difficulties.

At this point the design of the matrix had been thoroughly tested with students. It seemed clear that the mechanics were user friendly. More broadly, the interviews raised other important issues. Students wanted to know what kind of feedback they would get from faculty or advisors. This helped the project staff design orientation materials for the portfolio. Students also wanted to know if they could use the materials with potential employers, as "showcase portfolios." This request was repeatedly stressed to the University's IT personnel, and it helped them prioritize development of a "presentation maker" template that students could use before and after graduation.

Simultaneously with the student-side testing, faculty had been discussing the use of portfolios in general. Some faculty raised concerns about the conceptual task of populating a matrix with the entire array of documentation of mastery. Would students not take it seriously enough—would they upload items casually, hastily, even randomly? Would students take it too seriously—would they request extensive advising from faculty? Would they want detailed feedback?

Phase three. The spring 2010 student phase was designed to address these issues. Twenty paid volunteers were asked to populate the entire matrix, to keep track of how long it took, to ask questions of project staff as if to their advisors, and then to be interviewed about the process as a whole. This was still somewhat artificial, because if it were in full operation, most students would not be working with the matrix only in their final semester, but would fill it as they went along.

The findings of this final step were reassuring. Students reported that selection of artifacts was easy for most areas. They had the most difficulty determining what to submit for the stated outcomes when there was no specific core course that matched the area (i.e., technology and professional issues). Public library students reported the most overall difficulty determining items to submit. When asked about the usefulness of the ePortfolio, 65% reported that they saw value in measuring program outcomes, 60% felt it would be useful for job searches, and 35%, unsolicited, commented that it could be a tool used for evaluating teaching. Although it was stated that the function of the ePortfolio was for programmatic review, not individual student assessment, several students wanted feedback from the faculty on their ePortfolios. Students reported that it took them more than three hours to complete the ePortfolio—again, this was from start to finish, on an artificial schedule.

Overall, the three semesters of student testing resulted in:

- An interface that students found easy to navigate;
- An external/showcase option;
- Student appreciation for the ePortfolio as a measurement tool; and
- Instructions and assistance for students that was and would be manageable by staff or advisor faculty.

The student phase also resulted in a structure that was filled with items demonstrating mastery of 7 goals by 20 students. This constituted a small but viable aggregation of information that could be used for testing the next and essential part, namely faculty review of the artifacts for program assessment and improvement and conceptual and mechanical testing. That is, could faculty access the items easily? Did reviewing them provide information that made sense?

2. Faculty Testing

The task for faculty was to review student work, to determine the extent to which it demonstrated mastery of program outcomes, and to extract information that could be used for program improvement. The degree of mastery issue was framed as a mainly quantitative measure, while the process of program improvement benefited from a qualitative approach. Both were possible within this as well as other ePortfolio systems. For the quantitative measure, a reasonably consistent scoring system was needed. The other needed a way to note and aggregate observations about student work.

The first step was to access the artifacts chosen and uploaded by students. Oncourse, the IU learning management system, had reporting features that provided easy access to the submissions by learning objective and by student. Any authorized faculty user could click on a program goal, choose a report type, and be presented with a screen showing links (storage of) all of the submitted items for that objective, organized by student. By-student organization was especially important in cases where a student had selected multiple items to demonstrate achievement of the goal when no individual item would provide sufficient evidence.

In general, there are two complementary concerns in program-level evaluation systems—having enough, and validly representative material, and not having too much material for available faculty time. There are some better and worse answers to this dilemma. In some fields, such as nursing (NCLEX exam) and business (e.g., the ETS Major Field Exam) there are standardized tests that all students can be required to take. There is no grading time needed for faculty, and the data is reasonably detailed enough to be applied to program improvement, although the main drawback of standardization is the lack of local considerations. Another approach is to develop a collection of "best" papers. This is both easy and valuable for other purposes, but it ignores the range of students and student work.

Within IU's ePortfolio system *all* students populated their matrices of goals with artifacts. All students could use these artifacts to create "presentation" portfolios if desired, and any of them can request feedback from advisors. Not all items needed to be evaluated by faculty for program review, however. Instead, random samples could be identified that reasonably represented the whole, avoiding participation and selection biases.

Phase four. In the summer of 2010, each of the principal investigators in this study first looked at a selected set of submissions for one of the objectives to get an overview of the possibilities for review of the data. Qualitative notes were taken for each student, and then the investigators met to compare notes.

Technologically, preparing reports and downloading data was quick and easy. Both investigators found it relatively simple to determine whether a student met the stated objective or not, and they discovered that they had independently designed a rubric to assist with that evaluation. After comparing notes, a generic rubric format was designed as seen in Table 1.

The Oncourse matrix framework allowed for both numeric coding and text fields. The numbered scores for achievement allowed the School to generate brief broad summaries, and these also identified and screened for individual items which were scored particularly low or high, to ensure reliable ratings. Looking at overall averages, faculty reviewers then focused on identifying what areas had the best or weakest performance, and reviewed notes for those areas.

This was tested by using the rubric with additional qualitative note taking for a selected set of artifacts from two of the other learning objectives. Each student's cell took from 15 to 30 minutes to assess, based on the number of artifacts that had been submitted. For some program goals, many students selected the same course assignment to populate their cells, such as a final collection development plan assignment to demonstrate knowledge of the "Develop and manage library collections" objective. For others, there was a mix of basic and advanced course assignments (e.g., MARC records vs. digital library development plans). Students submitted one to five artifacts for each objective.

This pilot review showed a gap in the documentation. Each student had one overall program reflection. Sometimes this provided good information about how the student viewed their artifacts, but accessing it in conjunction

Table 1
Artifact Scoring Rubric

Student	Unsatisfactory (1)	Marginal (2)	Satisfactory (3)	Excellent (4)
A	Omitted part(s) of the goal	Included all parts but with poor quality	Included all parts at the level of basic coursework	Showed exceptional creativity and/or advanced knowledge
B				
C				
D				

with looking at the artifacts was awkward. In other cases students provided little detail, focusing on a very broad-level discussion of librarianship. Therefore, it was decided that it was necessary, when populating the objectives cells, for students to use a small comment field to provide a very brief description of why those artifacts were good—and complete—demonstrations of content mastery.

Phase five. At the beginning of fall 2010, Indianapolis faculty had their regular faculty retreat. Observations on student achievement based on the small pool of volunteers were shared among the full time faculty. Even this very limited amount of student learning data proved to be very interesting to the faculty, and provoked spirited discussion of what they could do in their courses, both basic and advanced, to reinforce program learning outcomes. This was the ultimate and very successful goal of program assessment, namely invigorated teaching, providing effective learning, and ensuring a continuous improvement environment.

C. Study Results

The pilot study explored the entire process of using ePortfolios for program assessment on a small scale, approximately 10% of full size. The final pilot data from 20 students was reviewed by 2 faculty members. This would compare to an actual annual review of data from approximately 200 graduating students by 20 faculty members when fully implemented. The pilot tested the entire process from start (student usability) to end (faculty use) to improve teaching and learning.

Interviews and data showed that the students had relative ease navigating the ePortfolio and determining what artifacts to submit for each stated learning outcome; however, the length of time taken to complete the process was longer than anticipated. The testers came into the study without previous knowledge of the ePortfolio, so in the future, this will likely be reduced by introducing all students to the tool during their orientation and by having faculty suggest certain assignments to students throughout their program that could be used to populate the ePortfolio.

Faculty analysis of the results was also found to be relatively easy. For the most part, artifacts submitted made it clear whether the student had mastered the content of the objective. A few questions did arise during the analysis. For example, students clearly presented information to demonstrate knowledge of the "Assist" component of "Assist and educate users of libraries and information centers"; however, the "Educate" component was weakly represented in the artifacts. Was this due to the students' use of "or" instead of "and" in reading the prompt? Or, could it be that artifacts were not a good measure for "Educate," because this might have best been shown in a live setting? For example, could observation notes be used as documentation? Or, was it not a measurement issue at all but an area where the program had a weakness. This was the sort of issue that could be examined in more detail with full implementation of the ePortfolio system.

IV. Conclusion

From this experience and the small pool of results, it appears that ePortfolio analysis provides a robust administrative framework and rich data for overall review of programs. It can identify problem areas, and faculty can look for causes which could include lack of coverage of the area in required courses, infrequent offering of an elective course in the area, or simply a flaw in the tool. If there were a problem with the tool, it should be adjusted. The real goal is to find and address weaknesses in the program itself.

Even in this initial stage, an example of use of the ePortfolio process, that is, identifying and addressing a problem area, occurred with respect to the program's technology outcome. One student near the end of his program submitted a simple PowerPoint presentation as the artifact to demonstrate knowledge in the "Demonstrate basic technical expertise" objective, and he stated in the reflection section that he consciously arranged his program to avoid technology-related courses. The fact that this emerged in the ePortfolio is a powerful demonstration of the importance of gathering information from all students, rather than (as is often the case), gathering only exemplary materials from outstanding students. At a faculty meeting, a consensus quickly emerged to integrate technology applications into more of the core/required classes, not leaving it to courses with technology "labels."

Informative data from representative students about program goals which is then used for improving the teaching and learning process is the purpose of any assessment process, and ePortfolios proved to be an effective, efficient tool for this essential academic purpose.

Each educational program designs its own outcomes and needs to tailor its mechanisms for assessment to the characteristics of its student body and its faculty structure. ePortfolios work well for students in distance/online programs with a relatively high degree of technological familiarity.

Acknowledgments

The authors gratefully acknowledge the assistance of Ms. Elsa Kramer in data collection and the Indiana University Purdue University Indianapolis Center for Teaching and Learning's "Integrative Department Grant" program for financial support.

References

American Library Association. (2008). *Standards for accreditation of master's programs in library and information science*. Chicago, IL: American Library Association.

Applegate, R. (2006). Student learning outcomes assessment and LIS program presentations. *Journal of Education for Library and Information Science*, 47(4), 324–336.

Billings, D. M., & Kowalski, K. (2008). Developing your career as a nurse educator: The professional portfolio. *Journal of Continuing Education in Nursing*, 39(12), 532–533.

Byrne, M., Schroeter, K., Carter, S., & Mower, J. (2009). The professional portfolio: An evidence-based assessment method. *Journal of Continuing Education in Nursing*, 40(12), 545–552.

Chitpin, S., & Simon, M. (2009). 'Even if no-one looked at it, it was important for my own development': Pre-service teacher perceptions of professional portfolios. *Australian Journal of Education*, 53(3), 277–293.

Fitch, D., Reed, B. G., Peet, M., & Tolman, R. (2008). The use of ePortfolios in evaluating the curriculum and student learning. *Journal of Social Work Education*, 44(3), 37–54. doi:10.5175/JSWE.2008.200700010

Gorlewski, D. A. (2010). Research for the classroom: Overflowing but underused: Portfolios as a means of program evaluation and student self-assessment. *English Journal*, 99(4), 97–101.

Hyndman, S. M., Gray, N. D., Pierce, M., & Hyndman, J. (2007). *From zero to over 2,500 eportfolios in six years: The Eastern Kentucky University experience*. Retrieved from http://www.usca.edu/essays/vol72006/gray/pdf

Klein-Collins, B., & Hain, P. (2009). Prior learning assessment: How institutions use portfolio assessments. *Journal of Continuing Higher Education*, 57(3), 187–189. doi:10.1080/073377360903263935

Kramer, R. (2007). Professional certification: The portfolio option: A timeline for success. *American Music Teacher*, 56(6), 66–68.

Mercer, D. K. (2008). Authentic performance assessment: Informing candidates, faculty, and programs. *Academic Leadership*, 6(1). Retrieved from http://www.academicleadership.org/article/authentic-performance-assessment-informing-candidates-faculty-and-programs

Palomba, C. A., & Banta, T. W. (1999). *Assessment essentials: Planning, implementing, and improving assessment in higher education*. San Francisco, CA: Jossey-Bass.

Scott, T. (2005). Consensus through accountability? The benefits and drawbacks of building community with accountability. *Journal of Adolescent and Adult Literacy*, 49(1), 48–59. doi:10.1598/JAAL.49.1.6

Shepherd, C., & Hannafin, M. (2009). Beyond recollection: Reexamining preservice teacher practices using structured evidence, analysis, and reflection. *Journal of Technology and Teacher Education, 17*(2), 229–251.

Suskie, L. A. (2009). *Assessing student learning: A common sense guide* (2nd ed). San Francisco, CA: Jossey-Bass.

Taylor, C., Stewart, L., & Bidewell, J. (2009). Nursing students' appraisal of their professional portfolios in demonstrating clinical competence. *Nurse Educator, 34*(5), 217–222. doi:10.1097/NNE.0b013e3181b2b530

Tubaishat, A., Lansari, A., & Al-Rawi, A. (2009). E-portfolio assessment system for an outcome-based information technology curriculum. *Journal of Information Technology Education, 8*(Annual), 43–53. Retrieved from http://jite.org/documents/Vol8/JITEv8IIP043-054Tubaishat710.pdf

Evaluating Teaching in Online Programs: Comparing Faculty Self-Assessment and Student Opinion

Gail M. Munde
Department of Library Science, College of Education,
East Carolina University, Greenville, NC, USA

Abstract

This chapter compares faculty self-assessment of teaching with student opinion of instruction in an online environment, in order to determine the level of agreement between faculty self-assessment and student assessment, in areas of overall program strength and directions for individual and whole-group professional development. A faculty self-assessment of teaching inventory based on established guidelines was administered to participating faculty in the Master of Library Science program at East Carolina University, and scores were compared to students' ratings of instruction for one academic year. Scores were corrected for bias, tabulated, and Pearson correlation and t-scores were calculated. The method used produced an effective benchmarking and diagnostic tool, and indicated directions for instructional improvement. Because the study was for the express purpose of internal, formative evaluation, model data tabulations are presented as examples only. Data from the actual study are not presented. Limitations of the study are that items on student evaluation of teaching surveys may not always lend themselves to concept mapping, and that data were collected only for one academic year in a single program. The chapter contributes a method that is replicable and scalable, demonstrates that data are relatively easy to acquire, and that procedures are simple to implement, requiring only basic statistical tests and measures for analysis. Results can be interpreted and understood without extensive knowledge of quantitative methods. There are few studies that compare students teaching evaluations with faculty self-evaluations, and none that specifically address it for library and information science education programs.

Keywords: Faculty self assessment; teaching evaluations; student assessment of instruction; best practices; online programs

CONTEXTS FOR ASSESSMENT AND OUTCOME EVALUATION IN LIBRARIANSHIP
ADVANCES IN LIBRARIANSHIP, VOL. 35
© 2012 by Emerald Group Publishing Limited
ISSN: 0065-2830
DOI: 10.1108/S0065-2830(2012)0000035011

I. Introduction

The vast majority of institutions of higher education in the United States require instructors to administer some type of teaching evaluation by students at the end of a course. Usually these evaluations are delivered as online or paper surveys composed of items that address significant aspects of effective course design and teaching, and include opportunities for students to comment on the course and the instructor. Although teaching effectiveness surveys are commonplace in higher education, questions remain about their use. Major concerns include low response rates and subsequent sample bias, and the potential effects of intervening variables unrelated to teaching and learning such as an instructor's personality, the amount or difficulty of work in a course, and students' actual or anticipated course grades. Nevertheless, student surveys of teaching effectiveness remain a presence in colleges and universities.

Most student survey processes are mandated at the institutional level, but used at the individual instructor level. Survey results are used in part to make personnel decisions, including performance evaluation, merit pay, teaching awards, appointment to graduate faculty status, reappointment, tenure, and promotion. They have been used less frequently as formative assessments or to determine directions for faculty improvement of teaching. Many faculty members would like to improve the effectiveness of their teaching, but may not know how or where to begin. In the online environment, student feedback can lack immediacy and there are fewer opportunities to observe student behaviors directly than in face-to-face classrooms. End-of-course student surveys may be the only opportunity instructors have to generate structured feedback. Faculty may be sensitive to their individual course evaluation reports and make course adjustments based on student scores for one or two survey items, but do not normally receive assistance in interpreting score reports in the larger context of identified principles for good practice in teaching. That is, instead of providing conceptual directions for the improvement of teaching, student evaluations most often result in an instructor making minor adjustments to improve scores on individual survey items. To broaden their perspective, 8 of 10 full-time Master of Library Science (MLS) program faculty members at East Carolina University (ECU) agreed to participate in a study to examine their student evaluations of teaching from a more holistic perspective, and to compare them with their personal self-assessments of teaching, both as individual instructors and as a group. Because the Department of Library Science offers its entire program online, integrated and systematic evaluation of the quality of online teaching is critical to overall program quality.

This chapter, after a review of the literature on students evaluation of teaching, presents a method to gauge teaching effectiveness using a framework by Chickering and Gamson (1987) that compares perspectives of students with those of their instructors. It discusses considerations for others who might undertake similar projects in their own settings. Because the study was intended only for the purpose of formative evaluation, actual study results are not presented. Rather examples of data tabulations and analyses are presented for illustrative purposes.

A. Literature Review

Overall, the literature on student evaluation of teaching is quite lively, and includes reports of rigorous experimental research and large national studies, in-depth meta-analyses of research reports, critiques of previous research, and personal essays and commentary. Interested and caring instructors often have strong opinions about the value of student evaluations of teaching based on their personal principles and experiences. The literature provides evidence for nearly any belief the thoughtful instructor might hold about the value of student evaluations, but empirical research shows the general practice to be worthwhile. Systematic evaluation of teaching by students has been considered particularly useful for identifying trends over time in large populations, and for identifying the ends of the curve, namely exemplary teachers and failing teachers. Given the scope of the literature, only a few examples are provided here to summarize the broadest general findings and criticisms. One of the most prolific scholars on the topic is Centra (2003) who concluded that

> No method of evaluating college teaching has been researched more than student evaluations, with well over 2000 studies referenced in the ERIC system. The preponderance of these study results has been positive, concluding that the evaluations are: (a) reliable and stable; (b) valid when compared with student learning and other indicators of effective teaching; (c) multidimensional in terms of what they assess; (d) useful in improving teaching; and (e) only minimally affected by various course, teacher, or student characteristics that could bias results. (pp. 495–496)

Marsh (1987) summarized the extensive research leading up to the development of the Students' Evaluation of Educational Quality (SEEQ) instrument:

> ... student ratings are clearly multidimensional, quite reliable, reasonably valid, relatively uncontaminated by many variables often seen as sources of potential bias, and are seen to be useful by students, faculty, and administrators. However, the same findings also demonstrate that student ratings may have some halo effect, have at least some unreliability, have only modest agreement with some criteria of effective teaching, are probably affected by some potential sources of bias and are viewed with some skepticism

by faculty as a basis for personnel decisions. It should be noted that this level of uncertainty probably also exists in every area of applied psychology and for all personnel evaluation systems. Nevertheless, the reported results clearly demonstrate that a considerable amount of useful information can be obtained from student ratings; useful for feedback to faculty, useful for personnel decisions, useful to students in the selection of courses, and useful for the study of teaching. Probably students' evaluations of teaching effectiveness are the most thoroughly studied of all forms of personnel evaluation, and one of the best in terms of being supported by empirical research. (p. 369)

Wachtel (1998) summarized a review of the literature on student evaluation of teaching effectiveness by noting that "after nearly seven decades of research on the use of student evaluations of teaching effectiveness, it can safely be stated that the majority of researchers believe that student ratings are a valid, reliable and worthwhile means of evaluating teaching" (p. 192).

However, the literature also reports many conflicting findings, and criticism of student teaching evaluations are manifest throughout. According to Emery, Kramer, and Tian (2003), the shortcomings of student evaluations were that they:

- are influenced by the popularity and personality of the instructor;
- they do not measure student learning or achievement;
- lack validity;
- are biased by small response sizes,
- are affected by situational variables not under the control of the instructor;
- are completed by unqualified raters; and
- are subject to errors in interpretation.

Fish (2005) recounts instances when student evaluations were used unjustly to harm exceptional teachers, and explains why he considers them "A whole lot of machinery with a very small and dubious yield." He maintained that

They are randomly collected. They are invitations to grind axes without any fear of challenge or discovery. They are based on assumptions that have more to do with pop psychology or self-help or customer satisfaction than with the soundness of one's pedagogy. (pp. C2–C3)

Algozzine *et al.* (2004) noted the difficulty of interpreting the body of research findings, but emphasized the practical and perhaps unavoidable reality of their use as follows:

Student evaluation of teaching is a very complex and controversial issue with inconsistent research findings. One thing seems certain: Student evaluation of college teaching is here to stay. It should be the duty of all individuals in higher education to continue to improve the evaluation process and to work toward providing a clearer picture of instructional effectiveness. (p. 138)

Several reports in the literature examine student evaluation surveys from the perspective of Chickering and Gamson's classic seven principles for good practice in undergraduate education (1987) and Chickering and Ehrmann's later explication of the principles applied to online learning environments (1996). Briefly, their seven principles are:

1. Good practice encourages contacts between students and faculty.
2. Good practice develops reciprocity and cooperation among students.
3. Good practice uses active learning techniques.
4. Good practice gives prompt feedback.
5. Good practice emphasizes time on task.
6. Good practice communicates high expectations.
7. Good practice respects diverse talents and ways of learning (p. 3).

Although these principles for good practice have been widely accepted as fundamental to successful college teaching, they are not often incorporated directly into instruments for student teaching evaluations. Achtemeier, Morris, and Finnegan (2003) analyzed 13 student evaluation instruments used for lower division core courses in online undergraduate degree programs offered within the University System of Georgia, and found that only two of Chickering and Gamson's seven principles were directly addressed, namely *student-faculty contact* and *time on task*. Only one instrument asked about *prompt feedback*. None of the other five principles were asked about in any of the instruments. Graham, Cagiltay, Craner, Lim, and Duffy (2000) evaluated four courses at using the seven principles as a framework for peer observation, instructor interviews, and discussion forum activity to identify strengths and areas where the school could focus efforts to improve its online courses. The results were presented in terms of the seven principles, but student evaluation data was not used as a variable. Zhang and Walls (2006) surveyed instructors of undergraduate online courses at a major university to determine their perceived use of the seven principles. Endorsement of the principles was measured by instructor reports on the frequency with which they employed each principle (*never, rarely, occasionally, often, very often*), and the results indicated that instructor endorsement varied widely among the principles. The least endorsed principle was *reciprocity and cooperation among students*, and the most endorsed was *communicates high expectations*.

II. The Research

Participants in the study were 8 of 10 full-time, tenured, or tenure-track faculty teaching in a graduate degree program delivered entirely online. They used a common course management system, but often supplemented their teaching with other online and Web 2.0 tools. Study participants believed that comparison of faculty self-assessments with student assessments could create a shared basis of evaluation with students, identify issues for individual faculty reflection on teaching, and serve as a departure point for selecting professional development activities for both individuals and the entire group. Research questions were:

1. Is there a statistically significant difference overall between faculty and student perceptions of the quality of online instruction according to the principles for good practice?
2. To what degree do faculty and students agree on the quality of online instruction according to each principle?
3. For individual faculty, and as a group of faculty, which of the seven principles would students score individuals and the group highest and lowest?
4. For individual faculty, and as a group of faculty, which item(s) on the Student Opinion of Instruction Survey (SOIS) will students score individuals and the group the highest and the lowest?

A. Methodology

Participating faculty volunteered to provide their individual SOIS reports from courses taught during the 2009–2010 academic year, and then completed a self-assessment inventory of their instructional activities that was based on seven principles for good practice. This self-assessment inventory combined elements of two available inventories, one developed at Howard Community College (n.d.) in Columbia, MD and a later version modified by the Lincoln University (n.d.) of the Commonwealth of Pennsylvania. Small structural and editorial modifications were made for the current study, with the largest modification being the addition of a rating scale. Prior to these activities, items on the SOIS instrument had been mapped to the seven principles and the mapping was reviewed by program faculty and received general approval, as did the self-assessment instrument. Student SOIS scores were compared to faculty self-scores across each of the principles for individual faculty members and as a whole group. SOIS scores were also analyzed separately for individuals and the group.

1. Student Opinion of Instruction Survey

ECU's Faculty Senate requires instructors, with few exceptions, to survey students in fall and spring semesters to determine their opinions of instruction. Survey administration is optional in the summer terms. The survey is referred to as an "opinion survey" to reflect the position that students may not be able to evaluate teaching effectiveness, but do have useful perceptions of the quality of instruction. In distance education courses students are sent a link to a distance education survey consisting of 18 questions about instruction, 6 demographic questions, and 20 about the use of technology. The18 items regarding instructional quality are:

1. The instructor created an atmosphere of helpfulness.
2. The instructor informed students about the criteria for grading.
3. The instructor made the objectives of this course clear.
4. The instructor was well prepared for each class.
5. The instructor demonstrated enthusiasm in teaching this course.
6. The instructor's course evaluation methods (tests, reports, assignments, etc.) were fair.
7. The text materials used were appropriate to the course.
8. This class challenged me to learn course materials, concepts and skills.
9. The instructor's syllabus clarified the expectations of this course.
10. The instructor provided the opportunity to ask questions.
11. The assignments (including reading, projects, and course activities) contributed to my understanding of the subject.
12. For the non-distance learning portion of this course, the instructor was available to students outside class.
13. The instructor provided useful feedback when returning tests and assignments.
14. The instructor demonstrated respect for me.
15. When applicable, the instructor provided different points of view toward the subject.
16. The instructor tested on the material emphasized.
17. The content of this course has been (level of difficulty on a scale of 1–7, with 7 being *very difficult*).
18. The amount of work/reading assigned in this course has been (demanding on a scale of 1–7, with 7 being *very demanding*).

Each item is scored by students on a Likert-type scale of 1–7, with 1 being *strongly disagree* and 7 being *strongly agree*. Except for items 17 and 18 (difficulty and workload), scores closer to 7 are considered more positive indications of the student's opinion of instruction. A score nearer the mid-point of the scale might be more desirable on items 17 and 18, and for this reason, these two items were analyzed separately. Students are best challenged by material that is not too easy and not too difficult, but slightly above the student's level of mastery. Less challenging work might bore students, while impossibly difficult work might dishearten students. Workload should be enough to cover course material thoroughly, but without becoming onerous.

ECU provides faculty members with an administrative report of SOIS results for each course taught. These reports include course mean scores on each of the 18 items, and the grand mean score for items 1–16, excluding item 7 (text materials). Because not every faculty member is free to select a textbook or other assigned reading (as in an introductory course where the text is adopted by an entire department or school), the administrative report does not include scores on item 7 in the grand mean score. Item 7 was included in the grand mean score in this study because MLS program faculty members were free to select their own textbooks and readings. The administrative report also provides a frequency table of the number of hours per week that students reported having spent on work outside of class, and the overall course response rate.

2. Faculty Self-Assessment Inventory

The self-assessment inventory used in this study (see Appendix A) was a modified version of an inventory prepared by Lincoln University (n.d.), which was initially developed by Howard Community College (n.d.). Both inventories were based on Chickering and Gamson's (1987) seven principles. Both were used with permission of their developers. The only significant non-editorial modification made for this study was the inclusion of a rating scale.

Lincoln University's inventory provided brief explanations of each principle and examples of how the principle would translate into action. When completing the inventory, faculty in the study reported here were asked to think about their teaching during the 2009–2010 academic year, consider the action examples provided in the inventory, and rate their performance on each principle along a 7-point Likert-type scale. Unlike the SOIS survey scale, faculty were asked to use a scale of 4–7, with 4 being *poor* and 7 being *excellent*. There were two reasons for retaining a 7-point scale, but adjusting the low end upward from 1 to 4. First, students use the higher end of the scale more frequently, that is, they assign higher scores more often than lower scores. Results of previous administrations of the SOIS, which included department and university-wide means in the administrative reports, confirmed an assertion made by Nulty (2008) that "In practice it is known that students' responses to questions on teaching and course evaluation surveys use the top ratings more frequently than the lower ones" (p. 309). Second, in addition to correcting for known student response patterns, retaining a 7-point scale, but at half-point increments (4.0, 4.5, 5.0, etc.), generated individual faculty self-score points that were more comparable to their respective averaged student scores, which were continuous data points (5.67, 6.20, 5.46, etc.).

3. Consent and Anonymity

In order to encourage faculty participation and reduce the potential for anxiety or discomfort, program faculty agreed to a set of study guidelines as follows:

- Participation would be voluntary;
- Faculty would not report elements of their individual analyses in personnel documents or discuss their results with others;

- Only one copy of individual faculty analyses would be produced and the respective faculty member would be the sole recipient of the report;
- The department chair would receive only the aggregated report; and
- The investigator would be allowed to submit a description of the study for publication.

Participants signed a written agreement to abide by these guidelines. The agreement specifically permitted the investigator to report details of the design, method, instruments, and statistical tests used in the study, but not the findings, results or related data. In order to promote faculty participation, such an assurance that participation would never be used to the disadvantage of a participant was considered a necessary trade-off. Because the results were to be used only for program evaluation, the study did not require institutional review of research involving human subjects, and this exemption was confirmed by the chair of ECU's Institutional Review Board.

To ensure anonymity of faculty self-assessment questionnaires and related student evaluations, each faculty member drew a numbered slip of paper at random, and wrote his or her name on it. The slips were handed to the departmental administrative assistant who placed them in an envelope and sealed it in the presence of faculty members. She held the sealed envelope for the duration of the study, opening it only to return completed individual analysis reports to the correct faculty members.

Faculty wrote their numbers on a return envelope provided, and enclosed their completed self-assessment inventories and their SOIS reports from courses taught during the 2009–2010 academic year. Identifying information, such as name and course number/title, was removed from the SOIS report sheets prior to enclosure. Sealed, numbered envelopes containing the SOIS reports and the coded faculty self-assessment were then given to the investigator. After the study, individual analyses, along with original faculty source documents, were returned to faculty members by the departmental administrative assistant who then destroyed the numbered slips of paper. A report of the aggregated results was provided separately to program faculty and the department chair.

4. Mapping SOIS Items to Faculty Self-Assessment Along the Seven Principles

Prior to data collection, items 1 through 16 of the core SOIS items had been mapped to the Principles for Good Practice. The alignment map is shown in Appendix B. SOIS items 17 and 18 (workload and difficulty) were excluded from the mapping, and were analyzed separately. None of the 16 remaining

SOIS items appeared to be associated with Principle 2, *reciprocity and cooperation among students*, so Principle 2 was deleted from the faculty self-assessment inventory. Not every SOIS item was a perfect fit with one of the six remaining principles. For example, Principle 4 encourages *prompt feedback*, while SOIS item 13 asks about *useful feedback*. SOIS items were mapped to their closest related principle, and the final mapping scheme was approved by the faculty of ECU's MLS program.

5. Data Analysis

One of the criticisms of using student evaluation data has been that low response rates bias the sample. Nulty (2008, p. 310) provided a table to determine minimum student response rates based on class size. Course sections with response rates not meeting the thresholds were deleted. The remaining data set met what Nulty described as "liberal conditions," which allowed for a 10% sample error, an 80% confidence level, and corrected for the tendency of students to respond at the higher end of the scale 70% of the time. Nulty noted that the table of required response rates "is, however, only a *guide* as it is based on the application of a formula derived from a theory that has random sampling as a basic requirement" (p. 309). Despite this caution, the present study sample was corrected for low response rates was presumed to include less error and bias than the total sample, and that student respondents were less likely to vary systematically from nonrespondents.

SOIS items had been mapped to the remaining six principles prior to data collection, and mean student scores from the mapped items were then averaged to produce a grand mean score for each of the six remaining principles. This score was compared to the mean faculty self-assessment score on the six principles.

B. Research Results

1. Agreement between Faculty Self-Assessment and Student Assessment

To determine the level of agreement between faculty self-assessment and student assessment of instruction across the six principles, a Pearson correlation was calculated between overall averaged faculty self-scores and overall averaged student scores on SOIS items as mapped to the six principles. The Pearson correlation for actual study data was .598 at the .05 confidence level, indicating a strong correlation. A tabulation with example data is provided in Table 1.

Table 1
Faculty Self-Assessment on Principles for Good Practice in Online Instruction, and
Student Opinion of Instruction—Example Data Tabulation

Principle for good practice	Faculty self-assessment grand mean	Student assessment grand mean	Gap/SD
The instructor encourages student-faculty contact and interaction.	5.25	5.75	.50/SD
The instructor encourages active learning.	6.20	6.50	.30/SD
The instructor gives prompt feedback.	6.50	6.10	−.40/SD
The instructor emphasizes time on task.	6.00	5.25	−.75/SD
The instructor communicates high expectations.	6.75	6.00	−.75/SD
The instructor respects diverse talents and ways of learning.	6.25	6.75	.50/SD

For example: r = X at CI;
t = X; df = X

Data in the example tabulation resulted in a weaker correlation of .341 between faculty and student scores, and reveals significant discrepancies between students' and faculty members' perceptions about "emphasizes time on task" and "communicates high expectations." Results such as these might indicate that instructors should focus more on activities that forward course assignments, for example, improving assignment pacing or scheduling, deleting course activities that are less related to assignment completion, closer follow-up of nonresponding students, asking more frequently for confirmation that students understand assigned readings, etc. Providing and using scoring rubrics for assignments, demonstrating skill requirements, and providing examples of excellent work submitted by past students might be ways for instructora to communicate high expectations to students.

The strength and direction of the correlation would be a general indicator of agreement between the two groups. A t-test of independent means was used to determine if the null hypothesis (there is no difference between faculty self-scores and student scores) should be accepted or rejected. The closer the t-score to 0, the more likely the null hypothesis is true and should be accepted. If the correlation were moderate-to-high, and the *t*-score did not exceed the threshold required to reject the null hypothesis, this would be taken to mean that faculty and students were in agreement on their respective evaluations according to the principles for good practice. That is, as a group of instructors, faculty members were likely to have a realistic perception of how well they were performing. The value of *t* for actual study data was .031 at the .05 confidence level, indicating that there was no significant difference between faculty self-scores and student scores. Nasser and Fresko (2006) studied the ability of 198 instructors in school of education at in Israel to predict their own scores on a teaching evaluation survey very similar to the SOIS instrument used in the present study at ECU. Among their conclusions was "The findings of our study showed instructor predictions of student ratings to be consistently related to actual student ratings; regardless of whether the overall course ratings or specific dimensions of the ratings (open-mindedness, organization, and stimulation) were examined" (p. 12). Providing a gap score (the overall student score minus the overall faculty score) would indicate which of the principles had higher or lower agreement, and could provide direction for areas in which faculty most needed improvement as a group. By also providing the standard deviation, the gap score could be interpreted with regard to central tendency. Negative gap scores indicate that faculty rate themselves higher than students, and positive gap scores indicate that students rate faculty higher than faculty rate themselves. Nasser and Fresko's (2006) research suggests possible explanations for such differences between perception and reality. For example faculty may be aware of student opinion, but in the name of modesty they lower their predictions. Another plausible interpretation is that these instructors are highly rated because they invest much in their instruction. They set very high standards for themselves, always feeling that they could do even better, and so are never really satisfied with their actual achievements (p. 13). To further examine areas of overall instructional strength and weakness, a simple tabulation of the grand mean student scores on each of the 16 SOIS items was produced, and item scores were rank ordered from highest to lowest. SOIS items producing the lowest scores provided insight into specific aspects of the related principles that might need improvement.

2. Workload, Difficulty, and Hours Spent by Students on Courses

On the SOIS survey form, students were asked to indicate the difficulty of course content and the amount of work, including reading assignments, required by the course on a scale of 1–7. For these items, a score nearer the mid-point of the scale might be considered more desirable than a score of 7 (*very difficult* and *very demanding*, respectively). The survey also asked students to estimate the number of hours per week they spent on course activities outside of class, presumably to clarify for instructors the students' perceptions of *difficult* and *demanding*. Students were offered interval response points, for example, 0–2 hours, 3–4 hours, 5–6 hours, 5–8 hours, and 9 or more hours. Taking the mid-point of the intervals, for example, 1 hour, 3.5 hours, 5.5 hours, etc., a frequency table was generated and Pearson correlations were calculated between hours spent and workload, and hours spent and difficulty. Both data sets were plotted on graphs to visualize the respective slope of the line, that is, if hours spent outside class increased as students' perceptions of workload and difficulty increased. Plot graphs with example data are shown in Figs. 1 and 2. The example data in Fig. 1 indicates that as the difficulty of course content increases, the number of hours students spend outside of class decreases slightly when the level of difficulty is rated higher than 5 out of 7 (with 7 being *very difficult*). The correlation coefficient for this data set is −.396 which could indicate that students become discouraged when course work is perceived as being so difficult that additional hours would not result in improved performance. Or, it could indicate that students believe that additional time spent on very difficult courses is not "worth it," in terms of other priorities. In contrast, the example data shown in Fig. 2 indicates that as the volume of course work increases, students respond by spending increased hours outside of class.

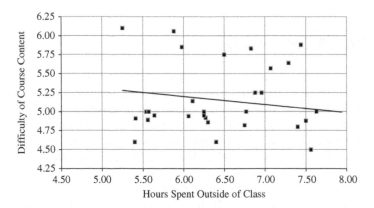

Fig. 1   Hours spent outside of class and difficulty of course content–example data. For example: $r = X$ at CI.

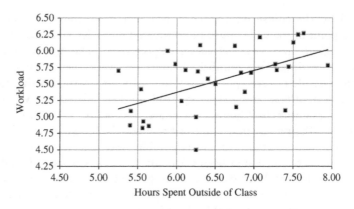

Fig. 2 Hours spent outside of class and workload–example data. For example:
$r = X$ at CI.

Therefore they may not be as sensitive to the volume of work as they are to the difficulty of work. The correlation coefficient for this data set is .538.

This analysis was a useful way to gain insight into the good practice that Zhang and Walls (2006) found to be most endorsed and used most frequently by faculty which was that good practice communicates high expectations. If instructors have successfully communicated their high expectations to students, then students respond to increased content difficulty and increased course workloads with increased effort in hours spent outside of class.

III. Overall Conclusions

If, as the evidence from Nasser and Fresko (2006) indicates, instructors are able to predict their own scores on students' perceptions of teaching effectiveness, then it may seem unnecessary to investigate further. However, this is akin to "teaching to the test" rather than asking instructors to evaluate their overall performance on established principles for good practice, which provides broader directions for professional development, both to individual instructors and to a group of program faculty. The design and method used by this study was found to be effective as a diagnostic tool. It indicated which of the principles offered fertile ground for instructional improvement through professional development. It also indicated areas of high achievement in terms of the principles for good practice. Although multiple measures of teaching effectiveness are encouraged by most institutions, little to nothing is systematically offered to individual faculty members beyond student evaluations of teaching and peer observation and review. This study, in attempting to compare faculty self-assessment with student assessment, contributes one more possibility to the tool kit.

A. Limitations

The study reported here has a number of limitations. Items on student evaluation surveys did not always translate directly into a principle for good practice. Many student evaluation survey instruments, including the one used herein, are derived from supporting research on the reliability and validity of individual dimensions—for example, preparation, clarity, availability, responsiveness, and knowledge of subject, that are known to be correlates of student achievement and overall student evaluations of teaching (Achtemeier et al., 2003; Feldman, 1996; Onwuegbuzie et al., 2007). Items on student evaluation of teaching surveys do not always address broader concepts such as those offered by Chickering and Gamson's (1987) principles. There may be other general frameworks or outlines of the best practices for college teaching, but Chickering and Gamson's are perhaps the most widely known and generally accepted. The sample used in this study, although large in proportion to the study population, is too small to generalize to other similar populations of online instructors and students. Data were collected only from two semesters, and this might not be enough to establish reliability. The study also required a measure of trust among participating instructors if, as in this study, the investigator is a peer member of the group rather than an unrelated third party.

B. Advantages of Methodology

The design and methodology of this study offered some undeniable advantages however. Data on student evaluation of teaching was routinely collected and made available to instructors, and data on faculty self-assessment was relatively easy to acquire. Participating instructors had the assurance of knowing that no one else would see their individual reports, and the advantage of seeing an aggregated report for comparison purposes. Both the aggregated and individual reports were used for formative evaluation only, which lessened potential fear of negative consequences among participants, and created opportunities for personal reflection and selection of professional development to improve teaching performance. The method and procedures were simple to implement, were scalable, and required only basic statistical knowledge. The results could be interpreted and understood by faculty in all disciplines, especially disciplines not centered in quantitative research, but whose practitioners were familiar with basic statistical procedures.

C. Recommendations for Use of Methodology

For other faculty groups who might wish to use or adapt the method and procedures to their own purposes, it is important to explain the process well in advance and to solicit agreement at multiple points along the way. For example, participants in the study at ECU had prior input into all procedures to be followed, approved the self-assessment instrument and the map of student evaluation items to the principles for good practice, and signed an agreement to participate that described exactly how the results were to be used and who would receive aggregated and individual reports. Faculty participating in the ECU study requested explicit reassurance that student comments would not be collected, as these were viewed as highly personal and often unfair, and if included might be a source of anxiety to the point of diminishing faculty participation. ECU's MLS program's Promotion and Tenure Committee was consulted and it was decided prior to implementation, that no data from the study would be included in documents related to its deliberations.

It was also useful to have the support of leadership throughout the process and afterward. There would have been no point in using this assessment to determine directions for group and individual professional development if there were no support for follow-up training and further professional development.

Appendix A: Instrument Used for Faculty Self-Assessment: Best Practices in Online Teaching

Principle 1: The instructor encourages student-faculty contact and interaction.

Frequent student-faculty contact is the most important factor in student motivation, intellectual commitment, and personal development. Interaction with faculty is a critical factor in online student success and satisfaction.

As an online instructor I: (consider all that apply)

- ☐ offer multiple forms of contact, including email, phone, online chat, and face to face, when requested.
- ☐ establish actual or virtual office hours at times when students will be available for online chats, phone calls, or email.
- ☐ acknowledge initial receipt of students' email with a reply.
- ☐ differentiate between types of inquiries (receipt of message, personal question, content question, procedural question, assignment feedback) and modify my response time accordingly.
- ☐ inform my students that infrastructure problems (server, etc.) are beyond the control of the instructor and may impact response time.
- ☐ create course assignments that build in feedback and communication (see Principle 3).
- ☐ make an effort to find out basic information about students.
- ☐ make an effort to introduce students to each other.
- ☐ refer to students by name.

Rate your performance on Principle 1 on the scale below

Poor   Excellent

4.0   4.5   5.0   5.5   6.0   6.5   7.0

Principle 2: The instructor encourages active learning.

To maximize learning, students must interact with the material they are learning, write about it, relate it to past experiences, and incorporate what they are learning into their worldview.

As an online instructor I: (consider all that apply)

- ☐ encourage student questions, input, and feedback.
- ☐ clearly state that all points of view are welcome and respected.
- ☐ regularly send announcements and general feedback to the whole class.
- ☐ follow up on students who are not participating.
- ☐ ask students to state what they expect to learn in the class.
- ☐ ask students to critique web sites that relate to the class and enhance learning.

- [ ] ask students to teach their classmates.
- [ ] ask student to develop/create learning activities and projects.
- [ ] ask students to review each others' work.
- [ ] ask students to reflect on their performance and their progress in the class.
- [ ] pose discussion questions that that foster critical thinking, problem solving, and extended and wide-ranging dialog.
- [ ] follow up reading assignments with discussions, simulations, or applications to case studies/scenarios.
- [ ] select real-world, relevant, and practical assignments that allow students to apply and practice the concepts learned.
- [ ] offer frequent short assignments/quizzes or other frequent "in progress" feedback opportunities.
- [ ] require students to reply and respond to online discussions topics.

Rate your performance on Principle 2 on the scale below

Principle 3: The instructor gives prompt feedback.

The instructor role is key, as it gives the students help in assessing their knowledge and competence.

As an online instructor I: (consider all that apply)

- [ ] respond with frequent email or discussion board comments: with answers to questions, comments about lesson/unit content, giving directions and information
- [ ] return tests, papers, assignments, etc. within 7 days.
- [ ] hold virtual office hours for students to discuss their graded work.
- [ ] post or send grades regularly.
- [ ] acknowledge all student questions.
- [ ] use grading rubrics to clearly and consistently evaluate student work.
- [ ] post outstanding student work and explain what makes it good.
- [ ] provide models of assignments (e.g., a model student essay or journal entry) to demonstrate expectations.
- [ ] follow up on feedback via email or phone if students do not respond initially to feedback.

Rate your performance on Principle 3 on the scale below

Principle 4: The instructor emphasizes time on task.

Learning takes place when time is used effectively and actively.

As an online instructor I: (consider all that apply)

- ☐ clearly define and explain course goals, performance objectives, grading and evaluation criteria, and give grading rubrics.
- ☐ indicate the relative emphasis of facts, critical thinking, analysis, reasoning, etc.
- ☐ establish and enforce deadlines for assignments.
- ☐ let students know how much time it should take to do the assignments.
- ☐ outline the steps for completing each of the assignments, breaking the assignment into smaller, more manageable parts if appropriate.
- ☐ use quizzes or questions that require students to review the content (either by students checking their own quizzes or questions, or the online quiz explains the correct response after students have answered incorrectly).

Rate your performance on Principle 4 on the scale below

Principle 5: The instructor communicates high expectations.

When the instructor sets high but attainable goals, academic achievement increases.

As an online instructor I: (consider all that apply)

- ☐ post a course description that clearly defines and explains course goals, performance objectives, grading and evaluation criteria, and indicates the relative emphasis on facts, critical thinking, synthesis, analysis, and reasoning.
- ☐ set high standards for myself and model lifelong learning through example.

Rate your performance on Principle 5 on the scale below

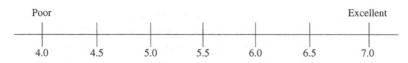

Principle 6: The instructor respects diverse talents and ways of learning.

Helping a student recognize his or her own learning style can improve a student's learning. Recognizing the learning styles of others can increase a student's repertoire of learning strategies.

As an online instructor I: (consider all that apply)

- ☐ design more than one method of assessment and demonstration of student achievement.
- ☐ allow students to choose from different possible modes of assignment completion
- ☐ encourage students to use the web and other resources and media to master course content by incorporating web-based assignments into the curriculum and reading assignments.
- ☐ recognize that distance education and online classes may not be the preferred or best learning environment for some students.
- ☐ am sensitive to possible cultural differences, especially communicating with students for whom English is a second language.
- ☐ design course materials keeping the access needs of individuals with disabilities in mind
- ☐ provide alternatives to reading text, such as audio explanations of complicated materials.

Rate your performance on Principle 6 on the scale below

Poor   Excellent

4.0   4.5   5.0   5.5   6.0   6.5   7.0

This is the end of the survey. Thank you very much for your response.

Appendix B: Instrument Used for Evaluating SOIS Item Alignment with Applicable Principles for Good Practice for Online Teaching

1. *The instructor encourages student-faculty contact and interaction*

   For example, offers multiple forms of contact, establishes actual or virtual office hours, acknowledges initial receipts of student email, differentiates between types of inquiries, makes an effort to find out basic information about students, makes an effort to introduce students to each other, refers to students by name.

   5.   The instructor demonstrated enthusiasm in teaching this course.
   10.   The instructor provided the opportunity to ask questions.
   12.   For the non-distance learning portion of this course, the instructor was available to students outside class.

2. *The instructor encourages active learning*

   For example, encourages questions, states that all points of view and welcome and respected, regularly sends announcements and general feedback, follows up on students not participating, asks students what they expect to learn, asks students to teach their classmates, asks students to develop/create learning activities and projects.

1.   The instructor created an atmosphere of helpfulness.

15.   When applicable, the instructor provided different points of view toward the subject.

3.   *The instructor gives prompt feedback*

For example, responds with frequent email or discussion board comments, answers to questions, returns tests/assignments within 7 days, holds virtual office hours, posts or sends grades regularly, posts outstanding student work, follows up when students do not respond.

13.   The instructor provided useful feedback when returning tests and assignments.

4.   *The instructor emphasizes time on task*

For example, clearly defines and explains course goals, performance objectives, grading and evaluation criteria, and gives grading rubrics.

2.   The instructor informed students about the criteria for grading.

3.   The instructor made the objectives of this course clear.

6.   The instructor's course evaluation methods (tests, reports, assignments, etc.) were fair.

16.   The instructor tested on the material emphasized.

5.   *The instructor communicates high expectations*

For example, posts a course description that clearly defines and explains course goals, performance objectives, grading and evaluation criteria, and indicates the relative emphasis on facts, critical thinking, synthesis, analysis, and reasoning. Sets high standards for self and models lifelong learning through example.

4.   The instructor was well prepared for each class.

8.   This class challenged me to learn course materials, concepts and skills.

9.   The instructor's syllabus clarified the expectations of this course.

6.   *The instructor respects diverse talents and ways of learning*

For example, designs more than one method of assessment and demonstration of student achievement, allows students to choose from different possible modes of assignment completion, encourages students to use the web and other resources and media to master course content, recognizes that online classes may not be the preferred or best learning environment for some students, is sensitive to possible cultural differences, designs course materials with the access needs of individuals with disabilities, provides alternatives to reading text, such as an audio explanation of complicated materials.

7.   The text materials used were appropriate to the course.
11.   The assignments (including reading, projects, and course activities) contributed to my understanding of the subject.
14.   The ECU instructor has demonstrated respect for me.

References

Achtemeier, S. D., Morris, L. V., & Finnegan, C. L. (2003). Considerations for developing evaluations of online courses. *Journal of Asynchronous Learning Networks*, 7(1), 1–13.

Algozzine, B., Beattie, J., Bray, M., Flowers, C., Gretes, J., Howley, L., ... Spooner, F. (2004). Student evaluation of college teaching: A practice in search of principles. *College Teaching, 52*(4), 134–141.

Centra, J. A. (2003). Will teachers receive higher student evaluations by giving higher grades and less course work? *Research in High Education, 44*(5), 495–518.

Chickering, A. W., & Ehrmann, S. C. (1996). Implementing the seven principles: Technology as lever. *AAHE Bulletin, 49*(2), 3–6. Retrieved from http://www.aahea.org/articles/sevenprinciples.htm

Chickering, A. W., & Gamson, Z. F. (1987). Seven principles for good practice in undergraduate education. *AAHE Bulletin, 39*(7), 8–12. Retrieved from http://www.aahea.org/articles/sevenprinciples1987.htm

Emery, C. R., Kramer, T. R., & Tian, R. G. (2003). Return to academic standards: A critique of student evaluations of teaching effectiveness. *Quality Assurance in Education, 11*(1), 37–46.

Feldman, K. A. (1996). Identifying exemplary teaching: Using data from course and teacher evaluations. *New Directions for Teaching and Learning, 65*, 41–50.

Fish, S. (2005, February 4). Who's in charge here? *The Chronicle of Higher Education, 51*(22), C2–C3. Retrieved from http://chronicle.com/article/Whos-In-Charge-Here-/45097/

Graham, G., Cagiltay, K., Craner, J., Lim, B., & Duffy, T. (2000). *Teaching in a web based distance learning environment: An evaluation summary based on four courses.* Technical Report No. 13-00. Indiana University Center for Research on Learning and Technology, Bloomington, IN.

Howard Community College. (n.d.). *Principles of best practice in the design and delivery of online education.* Retrieved from http://www.howardcc.edu/academics/distance_learning/faculty/bestpractices.html

Lincoln University of the Commonwealth of Pennsylvania. (n.d.). *Principles of best practices in undergraduate teaching.* Retrieved from http://www.lincoln.edu/imc/resources.html

Marsh, H. W. (1987). Students' evaluations of university teaching: Research findings, methodological issues, and directions for future research. *International Journal of Educational Research, 11*(3), 253–388.

Nasser, F., & Fresko, B. (2006). Predicting student ratings: The relationship between actual student ratings and instructors' predictions. *Assessment & Evaluation in Higher Education*, *31*(1), 1–18. doi:10.1080/02602930500262338

Nulty, D. D. (2008). The adequacy of response rates to online and paper surveys: What can be done? *Assessment & Evaluation in Higher Education*, *33*(3), 301–314. doi:10.1080/02602930701293231

Onwuegbuzie, A. J., Witcher, A. E., Collins, K. M. T., Filer, J. D., Wiedmaier, C. D., & Moore, C. W. (2007). Students' perceptions of characteristics of effective college teachers: A validity study of a teaching evaluation form using a mixed-methods analysis. *American Educational Research Journal*, *44*(1), 113–160. doi:10.3102/0002831206298169

Wachtel, H. K. (1998). Student evaluation of college teaching effectiveness: A brief review. *Assessment & Evaluation in Higher Education*, *23*(2), 191–212.

Zhang, J., & Walls, R. T. (2006). Instructors' self-perceived pedagogical principle implementation in the online environment. *The Quarterly Review of Distance Education*, *7*(4), 413–426.

Author Index

Subject Index